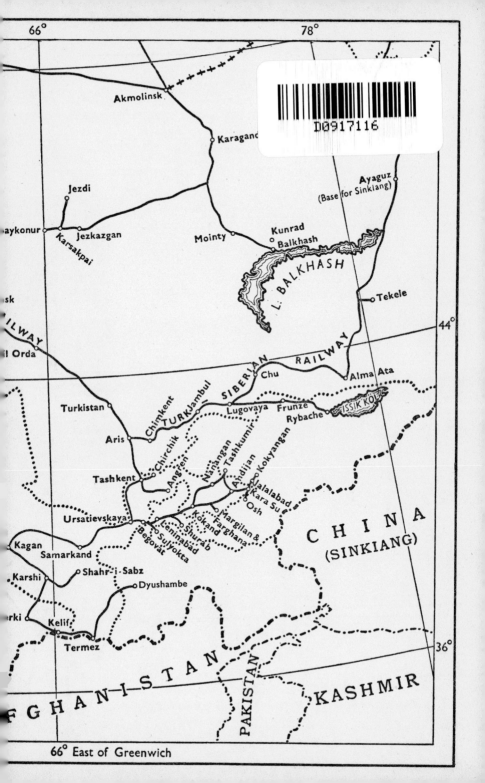

The British "Intervention"

in Transcaspia

1918–1919

Colonel Oraz Sirdar with Obez Baev seated on his right, and General Beatty and Colonel Alania standing behind

C. H. ELLIS

★

The British "Intervention" in Transcaspia

1918–1919

UNIVERSITY OF CALIFORNIA PRESS

BERKELEY AND LOS ANGELES, 1963

940.415
E47

Published in the United States of America by
UNIVERSITY OF CALIFORNIA PRESS
Berkeley and Los Angeles, California

Published in Great Britain by
HUTCHINSON & CO.
London

★

Printed in Great Britain

Contents

Illustrations

Line Drawings

Maps

Acknowledgements

Although the main facts of my account of events in Transcaspia and Baku during the revolutionary years of 1918 and 1919 are based on my own recollections, I am indebted to a number of former colleagues whose memories and impressions of north Persia and the Caspian area at that time have contributed to this study. Among these, happily still living, who shared my experiences are Major T. S. Jarvis (Malmiss), Captain D. Preston (Dunsterforce and Malmiss) and E. G. Longstaff, who was resident in Baku at the time of the British occupation.

My indebtedness extends to Colonel F. M. Bailey, on whose recollections of events in Tashkent and Bukhara I have drawn; also to Colonel G. E. Wheeler of the Central Asian Research Centre and Mr. David Footman of St. Antony's College, Oxford, from whom I have received much help and advice.

I am likewise indebted to the staff of the libraries of the School of Oriental and African Studies and the School of Slavonic Studies (London University), and the Royal Central Asian Society for facilities placed at my disposal.

Sources for historical research regarding events in Central Asia and the Caucasus are not easily available to those who do not command a knowledge of the Russian language. Although a number of works dealing with the so-called 'intervention period' have appeared in the Soviet Union of recent years, most of these suffer from their authors' need to conform to current theory or the approved 'party line', and are therefore unreliable both in their presentation of facts and their interpretation of motive and policies. I am therefore more than grateful for the painstaking research and careful sifting of facts relating to the history of the period evidenced in the recent works of Dr. R. H. Ullman, Mr. A. G. Park, Dr. Baymirza Hayit and M. A. Bennigsen which have greatly extended the range of my knowledge of the wider issues of Central Asian affairs.

I wish to extend my thanks to the Central Asian Research Centre for permission to reproduce the maps of Soviet Central Asia and Transcaspia.

Introduction

The events described in the following pages took place in Russian Central Asia, formerly known as Turkistan, a region that until the middle of the last century had become shadowy and remote in the mind of the Western world. Although there had been vague references to Central Asia, and to the peoples inhabiting its vast expanse of steppe and desert in the sixteenth-century chronicles of English travellers to Muscovy, it was not until the beginning of the southward Russian expansion towards the borders of China, Afghanistan and Persia early in the nineteenth century, undertaken at a time when Britain was engaged in extending and consolidating her rule in India, that Europe once more became aware of Bukhara, Khiva, Merv and Samarkand, cities hitherto almost as legendary as the Bagdad of Sultan Haroun al-Rashid.

By the eighties and nineties of the last century the writings of Vanbery, Curzon, Marvin and O'Donovan drew British public attention to Turkistan as a place whence the 'Russian Bear' threatened to descend on India. The position of Persia and Afghanistan in relation to the defence of India was the subject of frequent public and parliamentary debate in London throughout the last quarter of the century, a period in which the 'Eastern Question' and the future of the Dardanelles loomed large in European politics. The 'Great Game' (as it was called) of Anglo-Russian rivalry in Afghanistan, Persia and along the barrier of the Pamirs was a recurrent theme in the Press of the disputing parties and the subject of diplomatic exchanges between London and St. Petersburg. The ebb and flow of conflicting interests coincided with the ever-changing pattern of Anglo-Russian relations elsewhere, notably in the Balkans and what was then known as the Levant. Russian moves towards the Afghan and Persian frontiers, at times initiated by ambitious and adventurous soldiers and administrators in Turkistan with the secret connivance of the Imperial Court, and not always undertaken as acts of state policy, were regarded in government and military circles in India as another stage in the long-range Russian plan to seek an outlet to the sea in the Persian Gulf, or, by securing control over Afghanistan, to extend Russian influence to the valley of the Indus and beyond. Conversely, British moves in relation to Persia or Tibet gave rise to suspicion of British imperial policy.

Despite a certain amount of scepticism regarding Russian intentions on the part of some British statesmen, this view of the ultimate object of the Russian advance in Central Asia coloured the military policy of the Government of India throughout the last quarter of the nineteenth century. From the time of General Skobelev's descent on Transcaspia in 1881 and Russian moves towards the Afghan frontier several years later, the issue was kept alive until the Anglo-Russian settlement of 1907 defining their respective interests in relation to Afghanistan, Persia and Tibet eased the situation between the two governments.

The threat to India and the Persian Gulf had become less real after the defeat of Russia in the Russo-Japanese war of 1904–5 and the revolutionary outbreaks which followed. After the signing of the Anglo-Russian Convention in 1907 British public interest subsided until British-Indian military intervention took place in the Caspian area in 1918 and 1919, once more bringing the region to public notice.

The brief episode of the Anglo-Afghan war in 1919, and the former Turkish leader Enver Pasha's dramatic appearance at Bukhara after the Turkish collapse, occupied the headlines for a time, but an exhausted world paid little attention to these events or to the Basmachi revolt of the Muslim population of Turkistan against the Soviet regime. Enver Pasha's defeat and death attracted hardly any notice; even the Comintern's first serious effort to set the East aflame at the Communist-sponsored Baku conference of 'Peoples of the East' in September 1920 was not taken seriously by a public satiated with news of war and revolution.

Intervention by British-Indian troops in Transcaspia in 1918 and the temporary occupation of the great oil city of Baku by a British force from north-west Persia were actions that were to give rise to controversy that has lasted until the present time. These operations, primarily undertaken against Turko-German arms as part of a hastily improvised plan to block an enemy advance through the Caucasus towards India and Afghanistan, brought British troops into conflict with Soviet Russian naval and military forces on the Caspian and in Transcaspia.

They were, however, not planned as anti-Bolshevik moves, although their commanders took advantage of the opportunities presented by the existence of anti-Bolshevik and nationalist regimes in the Caucasus and in Transcaspia to pursue their military objectives. Nor did they arise from the traditional conflict of interests in Asia between Great Britain and Russia—the 'Great Game' of diplomatic exchanges and military moves and counter-moves that had exercised the minds of the political and military leaders of both countries for the best part of a century. As military operations, they were tactical moves, undertaken with the minimum of troops, to cope with an emergency brought about by the Russian collapse and an enemy advance eastwards in which involvement with the revolutionary and counter-revolutionary forces in Russian territory could hardly be avoided.

In the Soviet view, however, the presence of British and Indian troops in Transcaspia and the Caucasus was a deliberate act of aggression aimed at securing political and even territorial advantage at a time of Russian weakness. These small-scale operations were therefore regarded as evidence of British 'imperialist' policy; in other words, the 'Great Game' was still being played, the declared British objective being regarded merely as a subterfuge to disguise the real intentions of Simla and London. This viewpoint has been vigorously maintained by Soviet historians and propagandists until the present day.

Having taken part in the operations in Transcaspia and the Caucasus in 1918 and 1919, I was moved by two considerations in deciding to place on record the events of those troublous years in Central Asia. First, that this little-known military episode, hardly more than a side-show of the First World War, has become of considerable political significance in relation to the 'Cold War' and Soviet propaganda activities. Second, that in the absence of any detailed and authoritative account of these events by a participant, a completely distorted view of British policy and of the role of British forces in the Caspian area at that time—largely based on Soviet misrepresentation and unsupported assertion—has become widely current.

At a time when Soviet diatribes against 'imperialism' and 'colonialism' are the substance of their propaganda campaigns among the newly emerged Asian and African states, as well as in the corridors of the United Nations, it may be salutary to recount events which took place in an area in which the native Muslim population was the subject of the earliest Soviet denunciations of imperialism and colonialism—Tsarist Russian colonialism—and the right of self-determination.

The early Soviet attitude in relation to this question, and towards their own minority races, has undergone a considerable change since that time. Nationalism and the demand for freedom of subject people from foreign control are themes that are the stock-in-trade of Soviet propaganda abroad, but at home both sentiments are regarded as 'deviations' from Communist orthodoxy and even as crimes against the state.

My own participation in military operations in Transcaspia and Baku was fortuitous. After serving as an infantry officer for two years in France and Egypt I was posted to India, and in the autumn of 1917 found myself attached to a battalion of the South Lancashire Regiment stationed at Quetta in Baluchistan. Apart from minor brushes with Marri tribesmen along the Afghan frontier, this was garrison soldiering, but early in 1918 there were rumours of operations against gun-runners and raiders in Seistan in south-east Persia. A short period of service in that desolate and forbidding area was followed by staff duties in the course of which my attention was drawn to developments in Russian Turkistan and the Caucasus arising from the collapse of the Russian armies in north-west Persia and along the Turkish frontier of Transcaucasia. When news of the impending despatch of a British military mission to Meshed became known in the summer I volunteered, and on the strength of some knowledge of Russian and Persian (acquired to ease the boredom of garrison service) I was accepted and in July 1918 was posted to Meshed.

At this time some Indian units had taken over the duties of guarding the Persian-Afghan frontier region, hitherto the responsibility of Russian Cossack units which until recently had been stationed at Birjand, Turbat-i-Haidari and Meshed. A base had been established at the terminus of the Quetta–Seistan railway, and work was in progress in improving the road through the mountains and semi-desert country between Duzdab and Birjand, whence a Russian-built road extended to Meshed and beyond to the Russian frontier at Bajgiran.

The Mission at Meshed under the command of Major-General W. Malleson—consisting of three or four officers, a field-wireless unit and a small guard of Indian cavalry—was already installed in the old Consulate building. Contact had been made with anti-Bolshevik rebels against a Soviet government at Tashkent, and a relationship with them was growing up that was to lead to British and Indian troops being involved in military operations against Bolshevik troops along the Central Asian railway. The story of these operations and of the unexpected developments that followed is the subject of this book.

My original intention was to write an account of my own experiences during these operations, but after making a close survey of official and other records, and of recent Russian historical accounts of events in Turkistan and the Caucasus in 1918 and 1919, I decided to present the wider picture in as objective a manner as possible, basing it not only on my personal recollections but also on material in English, German and Russian which has become available since that time.

C. H. ELLIS

The Aftermath of the Russian Collapse in the Caucasus and Central Asia

THE seizure of power in Russia by the Bolsheviks in October 1917 was quickly followed by the disintegration of the Russian army. The Russian collapse not only freed German manpower for transfer to the West but also opened the way for German and Turkish penetration of the Caucasus and an advance towards Persia and Central Asia. Such an advance constituted a serious threat to British forces operating against Turkey in Mesopotamia, and ultimately to India. A hostile, if not actively belligerent, Afghanistan (already subjected to Turkish and German propaganda) would pin down large numbers of British and Indian troops which could be more usefully employed elsewhere. A shaky Persian government might be forced to join the Central Powers and become a base for operations against India.

The armistice on the Russo-Turkish front was almost immediately followed by the withdrawal in disorder of the Russian army, its arms and equipment being abandoned to the enemy or falling into the hands of the insurgent groups in Transcaucasia. Two Russian columns in Persia, one operating in the north-west under General Baratov, in co-operation with the British army in Mesopotamia which had recently captured Bagdad, and the other in east Persia, were also withdrawn, leaving the right flank of the British army exposed, and removing the barrier to the penetration by enemy agents into Afghanistan and India. Faced with this situation, British military staffs in India and at Bagdad had become acutely aware of the danger of a Turko-German advance through the Caucasus to the Caspian port and oil centre of Baku, and thence across the Caspian to Krasnovodsk and Turkistan.

With the conclusion of the Brest-Litovsk Treaty, the Germans entered into a separate agreement with the Ukrainian Rada, which had declared its independence of Russia. German troops occupied the Ukraine and the Crimea, thus gaining mastery of the Black Sea and the Caucasian coastal littoral. A German column entered the Caucasus at Poti, and having reached an agreement with the Georgians who had also declared their independence of Russia, occupied Tiflis. Turkish forces occupied Kars and Batum and began their advance through Armenia into Azerbaijan and north-west Persia.

The chief aim of the German Command was to secure Baku oil and the vast store of Turkistan cotton, both urgently needed for war purposes, while threatening the vulnerable British flank in Persia, and, via Afghanistan, India. Turkish aims seemed to be chiefly directed towards the fulfilment of pan-Turanian plans for uniting the Turkish-speaking and Muslim peoples of Azerbaijan and Turkistan under the flags of Turkey and the Caliphate.

Despite some conflict of aims between Germans and Turks, there was sufficient unity and co-ordination of effort between them to enable them to continue their advance unless effective resistance could be organized in Transcaucasia and Transcaspia. The existence of some 35,000 Austro-Hungarian and German prisoners of war in Turkistan, the remnant of a far greater number, now freed from restraint, constituted an additional threat to India in the event of an enemy advance along the Central Asian railway eastwards from Krasnovodsk.

In Turkistan a confused situation had arisen about which little was accurately known to the British authorities in India. A Soviet, Bolshevik in character, but supported by Menshevik and Socialist-Revolutionary elements, consisting of railway workers and returned soldiers, and entirely Russian in its composition, had seized power in Tashkent and other centres of Russian population, including the Transcaspian towns of Merv, Ashkhabad and Krasnovodsk. The Taskhent Soviet, acting as an autonomous body but taking its cue from the Supreme Soviet in Russia, proclaimed its authority over the whole of the Turkistan area, and having arrested or shot ex-officials of the former Tsarist and provisional governments, extended its administrative control to those centres where there was a substantial Russian population. Despite a declaration made by the Supreme Soviet in Petrograd in November 1917, which invited the Muslim peoples of Russia to organize their own affairs and establish autonomous administrations if they so wished, the Tashkent Soviet sought to prevent the development of any Muslim regional governments and, by decree, excluded representatives of the native population (which at that time comprised nearly 90 per cent of the total population of Turkistan) from any part in the government and public services.[1]

Cut off from central Russia at Orenburg by a Cossack force under the anti-Bolshevik Ataman Dutov, the Turkistan Soviet, often acting in opposition to policies proclaimed at Petrograd and Moscow, adopted a chauvinistic Russian policy towards the Muslim population. An attempt by Muslim Turkistani leaders, in accordance with the declaration of the Supreme Soviet in Petrograd on November 15th 1917, to establish an autonomous Turkistan government at Kokand, was crushed with great severity by 'Red' Guards, the city being destroyed and many hundreds of its unfortunate inhabitants massacred.[1] The survivors took refuge in the mountain country and the steppe, or in the still-independent Khanate of Bukhara, forming the nucleus of the so-called Basmachi bands which were soon in active revolt against Soviet Russian domination in Turkistan.[2]

Now faced with a widespread revolt of the Muslim population, and threatened by Ataman Dutov's Cossacks at Orenburg and other anti-Bolshevik forces in the north and north-east, the Tashkent Soviet began to organize a 'Red' Army, mobilizing Russian railway workers and troops recently withdrawn from Persia or former local garrison forces; also recruiting many Austro-Hungarian war prisoners who were given the alternative of enlistment or starvation. Although firmly entrenched in Tashkent and other centres of Russian population, the authority of the Tashkent Soviet was questioned by the majority of the native Muslim population, particularly in Transcaspia, where the rumblings of revolt had already begun to be heard in the spring of 1918. In Transcaspia the Turkman population, smarting under the high-handed attitude of the Soviet authorities, waited an opportunity to revolt. A deteriorating economic situation caused much dissatisfaction, and the local Russian railwaymen, mainly Socialist-Revolutionary in outlook, and perhaps more apprehensive than the Tashkent workers regarding the impending Turko-German threat from the other side of the Caspian, also began to display a determined resistance to Tashkent policies which was to culminate in the revolt in June and July 1918.

The failure of the Tashkent Soviet to recognize the threat to which it was exposed by the Turko-German advance can be explained only by the character and inexperience of the men who comprised it. Mostly railway workers, ex-soldiers and petty officials, their ignorance of the outside world was only exceeded by their revolutionary fervour. Ignoring the Turkish threat, already manifesting itself in pan-Islamic propaganda and intrigue, they embarked on a violent anti-British campaign, taking their cue from declarations made by Soviet spokesmen in Petrograd and Moscow, but also expressing the latent anti-British sentiment common to all classes of Russians in Turkistan, the outcome of suspicion and distrust fostered by propaganda in Tsarist times.

This atmosphere was being effectively exploited by German and Turkish agents. The propensity of Soviet historians to attribute to British intrigue the disorders of the revolutionary years in Turkistan may be partly due to propaganda as reflected in the local Press and Soviet public records of that time, but in the main it is an attempt to divert attention from the errors and high-handedness of the Turkistan Soviet towards the Muslim population.

It was in the light of these circumstances that the military authorities in London and Simla decided to send missions to north Persia to observe the rapidly developing situation, and, in the event of Turkish and German forces reaching the Caspian, to attempt to organize such local resistance to their further advance as was possible. In addition to these missions, a further mission was planned to proceed to Tashkent via Kashgar to establish contact with the local Soviet and ascertain what steps, if any, might be taken to deny the use of the Central Asian railway and cotton stocks to the enemy.

The first of these missions was 'Dunsterforce', a composite group of British officers and men under the command of Major-General Dunsterville, with a convoy of armoured cars, which left Bagdad for Enzeli, the Caspian port now known as Pahlevi, via Kermanshah and Hamadan in January 1918. This column followed closely in the wake of the retiring Russians, part of which force, a group of several hundred Cossacks under General Lazar Bicharakov, remained behind, having refused to obey the Soviet order to withdraw to Baku. The aim of the Dunsterville Mission was to secure the road to Enzeli and report on Turkish moves in the direction of Tabriz and developments in Baku, while at the same time to establish contact with friendly elements in Transcaucasia who might be willing and able to resist the Turkish advance towards the Caspian.

At this stage the British Command possessed little accurate knowledge concerning the situation in Transcaucasia. It was known that the Turks had formed a new 'Army of Islam' under General Nuri Pasha, and that this army, which had already established contact with Muslim leaders in Azerbaijan and Daghestan, was advancing towards Baku while another Turkish column was proceeding towards Tabriz. German and Turkish forces were in command of the railways leading eastwards from Erzerum and Batum. In the Persian province of Gilan a revolutionary band known as the Jangalis under the command of one Kuchik Khan, assisted by a number of Turkish and Austrian officers, blocked the road to Enzeli, acting as a 'Fifth Column' for the Turkish army marching eastward.

At Baku, where there was a large Russian and Armenian population consisting largely of oil and railway workers, a Soviet government had assumed power, but had little authority outside the city area, where the Azerbaijan Muslim population, although somewhat divided in its loyalties, was largely under Turkish influence. Krasnovodsk, on the eastern shore of the Caspian, and the terminus of the Central Asian railway, was in Tashkent Soviet hands. The merchant fleet, or that portion of it that was in southern Caspian harbours, wavered in its loyalties, but, on the whole, favoured resistance to the advancing Turks.

Opposition to Bolshevik control was, however, developing both in Baku and in the railway towns of Transcaspia. Conflicts between the various national and political groups—in Baku, Armenian Dashnaks, Azerbaijan Mussavatists, Socialist-Revolutionary, Menshevik and Bolshevik Russians; and in Transcaspia, Socialist-Revolutionaries, Menshevik and Bolshevik railwaymen, as well as Turkmans and Russians of all political creeds—absorbed the attention of the local population more than the threat of Turko-German invasion. The Armenians of Baku, who had already been subjected to pogroms at the hands of the Azerbaijan 'Tartars', were perhaps more apprehensive than others, being fully aware of the fate in store for them should the Turks and their local allies occupy Baku.

As the Turko-German advance through the Caucasus continued with little local resistance, tension between the various national and religious groups in Baku developed to a point where common interests gave way to racial rivalry. Local Muslim sympathy with the Turks could not be reconciled with Christian Armenian fear of their traditional enemy; anti-Russian sentiment among the non-Russian elements of the population developed as it became known, or was widely suspected, that there was connivance between the Soviet government and the German High Command in regard to the disposal of Baku oil.

The 'bourgeois' population of Baku, whether Russian or Armenian, having lost all confidence in the willingness or capacity of the handful of Soviet Russian troops to defend the city, supported the growing tendency on the part of the political parties (other than the Bolsheviks) to turn to the British in Persia for help.

During the spring and early summer of 1918 this question was debated in the Baku Soviet, all parties, with the exception of the large but already less influential Bolshevik group, eventually declaring in favour of an approach being made to the British as news of General Dunsterville's advance towards the port of Enzeli became known.

The Bolshevik group, led by Stepan Shaumian, an active and influential party man who had already played a leading part in Transcaucasia, acting under direct orders from Lenin in Moscow (with whom Shaumian was in close touch), attacked the British as 'imperialists', denounced proposals to secure British help against the advancing Turks and declared that the British objective was Baku oil. Despite all their efforts, the Bolshevik group continued to lose support in the Soviet and the confidence of a majority of the oil workers. They thereupon withdrew from the government, concentrating all their energies on underground agitation.[3]

Secret emissaries were sent to Enzeli by the Armenian 'Dashnak' and Socialist-Revolutionary parties in Baku, with the object of enlisting Dunsterville's help, but owing to delays in the British advance through the jungle country of Gilan, no contact was made until early June.

The second British Mission to be sent to Persia was the Military Mission under Major-General W. Malleson which left Quetta for Meshed in the Persian province of Khorasan in June 1918, arriving at its destination about the middle of July. The mission was later enlarged by the attachment of several additional Russian and Persian-speaking officers, two of whom had served as liaison officers at army headquarters in Russia before the revolution. A small detachment of Indian troops from units stationed in the Persian province of Seistan acted as escort and guards.

The Mission travelled by road from the railhead near the border of Baluchistan and south-east Persia. The road was little more than a rough track over the mountains and semi-desert of Seistan and Qainan. At Birjand, about halfway between the railhead and Meshed, two squadrons of British-Indian cavalry and a company of Pioneers formed the so-called East Persian Cordon, a small force patrolling the Afghan-Persian frontier region, and now being extended northwards to replace the Russian Cossack brigade which had recently been withdrawn from frontier guard duties between Birjand and Meshed.

The task of the Malleson Mission (known as 'Malmiss') was to keep a close watch on the situation in Transcaspia, to take counteraction against enemy agents endeavouring to penetrate Afghanistan and Baluchistan from the west, to keep an eye on developments in Herat and to take advantage of any possibilities of denying the use of the Central Asian railway to the enemy in the event of Baku being occupied by Nuri Pasha's army.

Aside from the activities of German and Turkish agents, the internal situation in Afghanistan was a cause for anxiety to the Government of India. In Kabul restless nationalists and reactionary mullahs, influenced by German gold and promises of help, agitated against the Emir Habibullah's policy of friendly neutrality towards British India. Pan-Islamic propaganda was rife, its influence extending to the North-West Frontier and the Punjab. This agitation was fostered by the Caliphat organization, a pro-Turk section of the Muslim community in northern India, which at that time, and later during the Afghan war, played an active part in disturbances in the Punjab and along the North-West Frontier province region.

Trouble in this area was, of course, unrelated to questions of world politics. Hitherto largely local in character, it was now linked with the growing Indian demand for independence. The political aspirations of the Indian Congress, coupled with pan-Islamic propaganda, and political and religious unrest throughout India, created a situation of exceptional gravity, intensified in northern India by widespread agitation and Turkish propaganda following the Russian collapse and the Turkish advance towards Persia and Afghanistan.

In eastern Baluchistan and across the Persian frontier in Seistan,

British military operations against bands of robbers, armed and supported by enemy agents, had been in progress during 1916 and the early part of 1917. These seemed likely to be resumed in the event of further Turkish successes and a Turko-German advance through the Caucasus, encouraging banditry and attacks against the British lines of communication between Bagdad and Enzeli and Baluchistan and Meshed. In central and southern Persia, the German agent Wilhelm Wassmuss, former German consul at Bushire, had stirred up the tribes against the British, and was still active in the province of Fars.

The railway in Baluchistan from Quetta to Nushki, completed after much argument between civil and military authorities in London and India in 1905 and extended to the Scistan border in 1916, had been planned as a counter measure to the building by the Russians of a line from Merv, on the Central Asian railway, to Kushkh on the North-West Frontier of Afghanistan, and to a threatened Russian drive to Herat and against Khorasan. For many years the building of the Nushki railway had been the subject of dispute between two official schools of thought regarding the national defence of India, namely the 'forward' school, chiefly military, castigated by its opponents for advocating a policy of 'mischievous activity', and an opposing party which was in turn charged with 'masterly inactivity'. Finally the military advisers won but only after a protracted struggle.

The threat from the north had subsided after the signing of the 1907 Treaty between London and St. Petersburg, defining spheres of responsibility and influence in Persia, and the railway had been little used for ordinary traffic. It now provided a means of communication and supply for the British-Indian frontier force in Seistan and the 'East Persian Cordon' in east Persia, and, as Malleson's Mission was established in Meshed, as the main channel of communication with the rear military base at Duzdab in Seistan.

Raids into east Persia and Baluchistan from beyond the Afghan border were now infrequent, but Afghan nationalism and fanaticism, stirred by the activities and financial support of a German agent, von Hentig, was awake, needing only a spark to start the flame of revolt. Thus far the Afghan Emir Habibullah had held out against the extremists, but the threat of revolt in Afghanistan and of disturbance on the North-West Frontier of India, coinciding with Turko-German penetration of Persia and Central Asia, was a serious one.

In the event of a Turko-German advance beyond the Caspian, the Mission in Meshed would be precariously situated, its line of communication with India being thinly held and in part traversing hostile territory.

Malleson's first action was to establish contacts across the border in Transcaspia with the object of denying to the Turks the use of the port of Krasnovodsk and the Central Asian railway. No immediate trouble was expected in Afghanistan, but within six months Habibullah was to die by the hand of an assassin at Jelalabad, and his unlucky successor Amanullah, in order to divert the fanaticism of his followers towards external objectives, was to embark, with Soviet encouragement, on the Anglo-Afghan war of 1919.

Major-General Malleson, who had served on the Intelligence staff of the Indian Army G.H.Q. and on Lord Kitchener's staff almost continuously from 1904 until 1914, was thoroughly conversant with conditions in Afghanistan and Persia. He had visited Kabul on Sir Louis Dane's mission to Afghanistan in 1904, and had made a complete study of communications throughout the whole Middle Asian area.

Apart from a short period as brigade commander in the operations against the German colonial army in East Africa in 1915 and 1916, Malleson passed most of his army career on staff and intelligence duties.

Among his colleagues he had the reputation of a somewhat dour personality with little interest in society or the lighter graces of an army career. His choice as commander of the Mission to Meshed was evidently due to his exceptional knowledge and ability as an Intelligence officer, rather than to his experience as a commander of troops in the field, a role that was clearly not foreseen in Simla when the project for sending a mission to north-east Persia was being considered.

Malleson moves into Transcaspia

WHILE the Malleson Mission was on its way to Meshed, a transformation in the situation in Transcaspia offered prospects of local co-operation in organizing resistence to the Turko-German advance into Persia and Central Asia. Towards the end of June Russian railwaymen on the Central Asian railway between Ashkhabad and Krasnovodsk struck against the imposition of a general mobilization order by Tashkent. For some time past there had been considerable local dissatisfaction with Tashkent administration, and the reported intention of the Soviet to transfer the railway workshops and headquarters staff from Transcaspia to Tashkent had aroused discontent on the part of local railway workers. Efforts made by the Soviet to pacify the region having failed, strong-arm tactics were adopted. There had been demonstrations against the Soviet at Ashkhabad and Kizyl Arvat, and local committees had been set up to air grievances. The Tashkent Soviet, alarmed by these developments, sent Frolov, the head of the newly formed Cheka, with a bodyguard of 'Red' Guards to Transcaspia to deal with the situation. On his arrival at Ashkhabad, Frolov, who had been authorized by F. E. Kolesov, a railway worker, who was now President of the Turkistan Soviet of Peoples' Commissars (Sovnarkom), to declare martial law if necessary, proceeded to do so. A number of people, including several of the railway workers' leaders in Ashkhabad, were arrested and shot.

The workers' committees were dissolved and a reign of terror was instituted. Having, as he thought, 'pacified' Ashkhabad, Frolov proceeded to the railway town of Kizyl Arvat, where news of his high-handed action in Ashkhabad had preceded him. On his arrival at the railway centre he was faced with a hostile and resolute body of railway workers, who, after a short struggle, shot him and several of his body-guards and disarmed the rest.

When news of this event reached Ashkhabad, the anti-Bolshevik revolutionary workers' committees reappeared and on July 14th a provisional government was formed. This consisted of the leader of the Ashkhabad revolt, T. Funtikov, a Socialist-Revolutionary worker, Vladimir Dokhov and D. Kurilov, both railwaymen, and L. A. Zimen, a schoolmaster.

Funtikov was appointed President of the Executive Committee (as the government was called), with Zimen as Minister for Foreign Affairs, the other members dividing ministerial responsibilities between them. Funtikov, an energetic and ruthless character, seemed to have few other qualifications for leadership of a government, and indeed, apart from Zimen, who was an educated man and something of an orientalist, none of them had any experience of public affairs.

The revolts at Ashkhabad and Kizyl Arvat were quickly followed up by uprisings at Krasnovodsk and Merv. An improvised defence force seized Merv a week later, while at Krasnovodsk a *stachkom* or strike committee, under a Caucasian officer, Kuhn, accepted direction from Ashkhabad, and, having seized control of the town and port, ousted the Bolshevik authorities there.

The Ashkhabad Committee then proceeded to take revenge for the shooting of Socialist-Revolutionary and Menshevik leaders by Frolov, and with very little ceremony shot the Bolshevik Commissars who had been arrested at Merv, Kizyl Arvat and Krasnovodsk, as well as a number of the leading Bolsheviks in Ashkhabad itself.

Having burnt its boats by this action, the Ashkhabad Committee had no alternative to surrender but to defend itself against the inevitable onslaught from the 'Red' forces of Tashkent. A number of ex-officers, including a former general of the Tsarist army, General Krutin, immediately proffered their services, and a few hundred ex-soldiers, as well as remnants of the 'Red' Guard troops who had gone over to the anti-Bolshevik government, were enrolled.

Very little military equipment was available, and practically no artillery. The main store of guns and ammunition was at Kushkh, the fortress on the Afghan frontier, south of Merv, but its garrison having declared for the Bolshevik regime, it was too strong to be overcome by the military force available to the Ashkhabad government.

Armoured trains were hastily improvised with bales of cotton to protect gun-crews, and the little army, with no cavalry to protect its flanks, moved up the line towards the rail crossing of the river Amu-Darya (Oxus) at Chardzhou. By July 24th a position had been taken astride the railway at Repetek, a few miles south-west of the river-crossing. Colonel Oraz Sirdar, the Transcaspian commander, aimed at seizing the bridge and destroying it, and entertained a vain hope that help might be forthcoming from the Emir of Bukhara, at that time on unfriendly terms with the Soviet at Tashkent.[1]

Although taken by surprise by events in Transcaspia, the Tashkent authorities were quick to act. A Military Commissariat and a Politico-Military staff were improvised, and additional 'Red' Army regiments were hastily formed in which railway workers and many ex-prisoners of war, mainly Hungarians, were enrolled. Armoured trains, protected by steel plates and bales of cotton and armed with field guns, adapted for the purpose, were quickly assembled.

On the morning of July 24th the 'Red' Army, having occupied Chardzhou and now in possession of the railway bridge, attacked in force, driving the Transcaspians back to Uchaji, and thence to a position several miles east of Bairam Ali, covering the Merv oasis.

The attitude of the Turkman tribes in Transcaspia thus far had been uncertain. Strongly anti-Russian, and now influenced by Turkish propaganda, at first they displayed no strong disposition to support the new government in Ashkhabad. Their hatred of the Bolsheviks, at whose hands they had suffered many indignities, was, however, greater than their fear and dislike of Russians in general, and several of their leaders, notably Colonel Oraz Sirdar, a Turkman officer of the Tsarist army, Obez Baev and Hadji Murat, all educated men, favoured giving pro-visional support to the new regime. Although suspicious of the Turk-man leaders, the Executive Committee had no alternative but to come to terms with them, and in return for several thousand rifles and a considerable sum of money they undertook to provide cavalry units for service at the front. Some of these Turkman units had already reached Merv where they were settling old scores. Under Oraz Sirdar's leadership, however, steps were taken to move some of these horsemen to the front, where cavalry was badly needed to screen the flanks of the vulnerable armoured trains.

General Malleson, who had been fully informed of these develop-ments by Intelligence agents who had preceded the Mission and had visited Transcaspia and Baku in the role of Persian traders, sent one of his officers to a point on the Persian-Transcaspian frontier near Muhammedabad to report on the situation. As a precautionary measure he ordered a company of the 19th Punjabis, then stationed at Birjand, to proceed to the frontier and establish a line of communications between the zone of operations along the Central Asian railway and Meshed.

Up to the middle of July the attitude of the Government of India and the War Office in London to the possibility of British forces being engaged in operations on Russian territory was one of indecision. General Dunsterville, who had arrived at Enzeli, after a brush with the Jangalis, sought authority to send a reconnaisance party to Baku but thus far had been denied permission. Representatives of the 'Dashnak' party in Baku had established contact with his advance party at Resht, and had requested British help in organizing resistance to the approaching Turks.[2]

So far, both London and Simla had shown reluctance to become militarily involved in the turmoil beyond the northern Persian border. Dunsterville's main task had been achieved in securing the road from Hamadan to Kazvin and establishing a defence line between Kazvin and the Caspian port of Enzeli (since renamed Pahlevi). Although thinly held with a precarious line of communication to Bagdad, the existence of a British force screening Tehran from the depredations of the Jangalis and the Turkish advance guards gave courage to the weak and vacillating Persian government which had been on the point of collapse.

By occupying Enzeli and obtaining control of a number of ships at this port, Dunsterville was well placed to observe developments in Baku, and at the same time to take steps in collaboration with Malleson to prevent the port of Krasnovodsk and the Central Asian railway falling into enemy hands.

Malleson's instructions contained no provision for military intervention in Transcaspia, although he had been given *carte blanche* to devise means to hold up a Turko-German advance along the railway. Without troops at his disposal, other than a small detachment from the East Persian Cordon, and limited financial resources, his first duty was to avoid the risks of physical involvement. Yet the changed situation in Transcaspia and the possibilities for rendering the railway useless to the Turks and preventing the store of Turkistan cotton falling into enemy hands, now presented by the Transcaspian revolt against Tashkent, urged him to recommend that the risk be accepted if his help was sought by the Ashkhabad Committee, as now seemed likely.

Early in August contact had already been established with the Transcaspian authorities. Malleson's representative at Muhammedabad had already been approached by officers of Oraz Sirdar's command, and tentative inquiries were now being made by agents of the Ashkhabad Committee as to the possibility of British military and financial assistance being made available. Alarmed by the defeat of their troops near Bairam Ali, the Ashkhabad Committee, feeling themselves unable to cope with the consequences of their own action, and now on the defensive in face of a threatened attack on Merv, decided to make a formal approach to the Malleson Mission. When informed of the Committee's intention, General Malleson despatched a liaison officer, Captain Teague-Jones, to Ashkhabad with authority to enter into discussions with the Transcaspian authorities for the conclusion of an agreement, whereby, in return for their taking steps to improve the defences of Krasnovodsk and, if necessary, to render the Central Asian railway useless for the transport of enemy traffic, some British assistance would be forthcoming.

In making this proposal to Ashkhabad, General Malleson availed himself of the 'free hand' accorded to him by the authorities at Simla. In reply to his report to headquarters in India regarding his proposed course of action he was instructed by the Commander-in-Chief, General Munro, to sound out the new regime in Transcaspia and make whatever arrangements with them he deemed necessary to deal with the emergency that had arisen. No offer of reinforcements from India was made and no additional funds were made available for the purpose, a circumstance that was to give rise to considerable difficulty at a later date.[3]

Malleson immediately took steps to survey the road between Meshed and Bajgiran on the Transcaspian frontier, and to bring up reinforcements from the East Persian Cordon, in the shape of the 28th Indian Cavalry Regiment, and two more companies of the 19th Punjabis from Birjand.

Agreement in principle having been reached with very little delay in the preliminary talks in Ashkhabad, arrangements were made to reinforce the detachment of Indian troops at Muhammedabad. A further retreat by the Transcaspians to Bairam Ali, after several engagements in which casualties had been high on both sides, was followed by an urgent appeal to Malleson from Ashkhabad for immediate help. The loss of Merv and the surrounding irrigated area was a severe blow to Ashkhabad which depended on the resources of the area for food supplies. Moreover, the railway from Merv to Kushkh was now in Bolshevik hands, enabling them to draw on stocks of artillery, ammunition and other supplies in the Kushkh fortress.

On August 8th Malleson was authorized by headquarters in India to afford limited military and financial assistance to the Transcaspian government. So far, however, the War Office in London had confined itself to taking note of Malleson's moves. On the 10th the company of infantry and a machine-gun section crossed the frontier at Muhamme-dabad to Artyk, a station on the Central Asian railway. To aid the now hard-pressed Transcaspian army, the British-Indian machine-gun section was sent up the line with orders to assist Colonel Oraz Sirdar in consolidating a new position astride the railway.

On August 13th the Tashkent 'Red' forces attacked, driving the defenders, who took to the armoured trains, back to Dushakh, nearly 100 miles to the rear. The British machine-gun section later joined the defenders at this point, playing an active part in covering a further retreat several days later to a more defensible position at Kaakha.

The action at Dushakh, although little more than a skirmish, brought British and Indian forces into conflict with Russians in Central Asia for the first time.

During the last quarter of the nineteenth century, and in the early years of the present century, the possibility of Russian and British forces meeting along the Afghan or Persian frontiers with Russian Turkistan was a frequent theme of political writers. Such a possibility no doubt exercised the minds of military strategists and planners on both sides, and while the Foreign Offices of London and St. Petersburg were undoubtedly actuated by a sincere desire to restrain the ambitions or allay the fears of general staffs, the planning and construction of railways and roads in Turkistan, Persia and Baluchistan had been undertaken with this possibility in view. After the Anglo-Russian Agreement of 1907 the apparent danger had receded, the threat of war from other quarters drawing official and public attention elsewhere.

By 1914 it seemed unlikely that the conflict would be resumed in the near future. In the event, the action at Dushakh did not arise from Anglo-Russian rivalry but from largely fortuitous circumstances stemming from the advance of a common enemy, the Turko-German invaders of Persia and Transcaucasia.

While these operations were in progress the wretched population of Merv and Tedzhen had suffered from depredations by both sides, as well as from the attentions of a local Turkman bandit, Aziz Khan. This man, formerly an important personage (in his own estimation) in the Tedzhen oasis, had until recently lived in retirement in Afghanistan, and was believed to be acting in collusion with ambitious politicians in that country. Taking advantage of the prevailing disorder, he had descended on Tedzhen, robbing and murdering its inhabitants. With the return of the Bolsheviks, he withdrew beyond the frontier, doubtless awaiting an opportunity to renew his brigandage. Aziz Khan, who met the end he deserved at the hands of the Ashkhabad Committee some months later, was a thorn in the flesh to friend and foe, and has won spurious renown in Soviet historical accounts of the period by being represented as a British agent, a role he certainly never played.

In the meantime the Ashkhabad Committee sent one of its members, Dokhov, to Meshed to complete the negotiations for an agreement, which was formally reached and signed on August 19th.

3

Dunsterville at Baku

AT THE time these events were taking place in Transcaspia a parallel situation had developed in Baku. The Bolshevik group which had hitherto dominated the Baku Soviet had resigned, and a new government, known as the 'Centro-Caspian Directorate' in which Dashnaks and Socialist-Revolutionaries predominated, followed up its tentative approach to General Dunsterville, formally requesting his assistance in men and equipment for the organization of a defence force.[1]

The change-over in Baku took place within a few days of the revolt of the railwaymen against Tashkent in Kizyl Arvat and Ashkhabad and the formation of a new government in Transcaspia. Malleson and Dunsterville had been keeping each other informed, via India and Tehran, but, as we have seen, their initiative was to some extent hampered by the reluctance of the authorities in London to agree to British troops becoming involved in operations beyond the Persian frontiers.

The force at General Dunsterville's disposal, although now reinforced by several companies of infantry, some light artillery and armoured cars, was quite inadequate to undertake a full-scale defence of Baku. However, by agreement with the Baku government, General Bicharakov's Cossacks were shipped from Enzeli to Baku to form part of the defence line, and several merchant ships belonging to the Russian Caspian merchant fleet were taken over by Dunsterville and armed as auxiliary cruisers.

By the end of July Dunsterville was authorized to send a reconnaissance party to Baku, and to enter into discussions with the Centro-Caspian government for an agreement for British help in defending Baku against the Turks. In the absence of any unity of command the military force at the disposal of the Baku government, although substantial in numbers, was clearly incapable of withstanding a determined attack. It was hoped that by providing better leadership and training

C

and raising the morale of the troops that an effective force could be formed. These hopes were to be disappointed, owing to the lack of discipline and unwillingness to fight displayed by both Armenian and Russian troops, but in the meantime Krasnovodsk was safe from attack by Soviet forces from Astrakhan, and a naval force under British command had been brought into being.

A small British advance party left Enzeli on August 4th for Baku to undertake a reconnaissance of the military situation and to ascertain what military stores and equipment were in the Baku arsenal.

It had been made clear to the agents of the Baku government that no large British force could be made available for the defence of the city, but that some arms and equipment might be supplied as well as a small detachment of troops and instructors for the training and organization of local forces. It was known that considerable supplies of arms were stored in Baku, and that these had not been placed at the disposal of any single force ostensibly because of the absence of a central military command. In fact the failure to make military stores available was largely due to the political and racial jealousy and fears that hampered the work of organized government in the distracted city.[2]

The most Dunsterville could do with the meagre resources at his disposal would be to plan and organize the defence, and stiffen the mixed forces of the Baku authorities with a few hundred British infantry and gunners. At that time about 2,500 Soviet Russian troops still occupied the line of defence, although maintaining their independence of command. Soviet official policy in relation to the German and Turkish advance in the Caucasus was apparently still undecided in Moscow, negotiations between the Soviet and German governments over the question of oil and other matters not having yet been completed. The part that Soviet Russian troops would play in defence of the city was uncertain, but the clamour against alleged British and American designs on Baku oil, emanating from Moscow, suggested that the harassed Soviet government, although anxious to prevent the city and oil fields falling into Turkish hands, was more concerned with ideological considerations and with its anti-British agitation in Asia than in taking practical steps to safeguard a key point of such vital importance as Baku.

Information was now being received from Tiflis and Vladikavkaz regarding German plans in the Caucasus. The German commander in

Tiflis, General Kress von Kressenstein, had entered into an agreement with the Menshevik government of Georgia, which had undertaken to provide the Germans with manganese and other minerals, seeking in return to secure German support against the Turks who were encroaching on Georgian territory. Negotiations were also being conducted between Georgian emissaries and the German Foreign Office in Berlin.[3]

Towards the end of July one of the Georgian representatives, Avalishvili, who had been sent to Berlin, visited Oslo, where he got into touch with the British and French Ambassadors, informing them of the discussions in Berlin, and of German negotiations with Moscow for the supply to the Germans of oil and cotton. The Georgians wished to convey to the Allied governments that their relations with the Germans were dictated by necessity, and did not imply hostility to the Allies.[4]

The action of the Bolshevik Commissars in withdrawing from the Baku government, the ambiguous attitude of Bolshevik Russian military commanders and the arrival of a German mission in Baku, coupled with the information now being received by the British from Tiflis and Oslo, all pointed towards collusion between Berlin and Moscow. Moreover, German efforts to restrict Turkish movements, while pursuing their own aims, supported persistent reports of the conclusion of a deal between Moscow and Berlin to give the Germans access to Baku oil and Turkistan cotton.

The permission given to General Dunsterville at the beginning of August to accept the invitation of the Centro-Caspian government in Baku was accorded by the authorities in London and Simla in recognition of the gravity of the situation as disclosed by the latest information regarding German and Turkish plans and Soviet discussions with Berlin.

Tentative plans to deploy part of Dunsterville's force in the direction of Tabriz were now postponed, and arrangements were made in Bagdad to reinforce the troops in Enzeli and along the Hamadan–Kazvin–Enzeli road. In recognition of the fact that enemy control over Caspian shipping would enable the Turks to continue their advance into Transcaspia and north Persia, Dunsterville had taken steps to form the nucleus of a Caspian naval force by arming several merchant ships.

He now entered into negotiation with the Baku government to make other ships available and to build up a reserve of oil fuel and stores at Enzeli and Krasnovodsk, and arranged with Malleson for joint action in defending Krasnovodsk against attack from Astrakhan or Baku.

The outlook at Baku had not improved. While Dunsterville's representatives in Baku were endeavouring to persuade the Baku government to strengthen the natural defences of the city, in view of the absence of any unity of command over the local troops, and the unreliability of these forces, largely Armenian, there seemed to be little prospect of holding off the Turkish attack. Precautionary steps had been taken to hold several ships in the Baku harbour for the eventual withdrawal of the British force should this prove necessary.

At the time of arrival of the first British detachments under Colonel C. B. Stokes on August 4th, the total strength of the local troops nominally under the command of the Baku government was about 8,000, including nearly 3,000 Soviet Russian infantry and artillery, about half of which had recently arrived from Astrakhan under a Soviet General, Petrov. Bicharakov's cavalry, which had been operating on the left flank of the defence line, had met with difficulties in regard to supply and co-ordination of command, and had withdrawn northward. The main body of the Baku army consisted of Armenians, some volunteers, but the majority conscripted men.

Of the extremely mixed population of Baku, the Armenians had most to fear from the Turks. The loyalties of the 'Tartars' were divided; most were pro-Turk, but in general they stood for Azerbaijan independence. The pro-Bolshevik Russians sought to maintain the Russian connection and took their orders from Moscow, while the attitude of the rest of the population mainly concerned about their personal affairs, seemed undecided. After the withdrawal of the Bolsheviks from the Baku Soviet, and the establishment of the Centro-Caspian Directorate on July 31st, Soviet Russian troops no longer took an active part in the defence arrangements. A further detachment arrived from the north a few days later, but after an unsuccessful attempt to stir up the local population against the new government, the Russians, seemingly on instructions from Moscow, decided to withdraw. On August 12th the Soviet Russian force, accompanied by the Bolshevik members of the former government, sailed for Astrakhan in twelve ships which had been placed at their disposal by the Baku authorities.

When it was discovered that a considerable part of the contents of the Baku arsenal had been removed and shipped away, the ships were intercepted by armed vessels of the new government and forced to return to Baku. The military stores were unloaded and the Soviet Commissars placed under arrest. The ships and Soviet troops were then allowed to depart and made their way unmolested to Astrakhan.

The withdrawal of the Soviet Russian troops from Baku completely alienated even that section of the population, chiefly oil and railway workers, which had so far supported the Soviet, and popular approval of the new government's policy of seeking British support was now overwhelming, despite the differences of opinion between the various parties and the antagonism between the Armenian and Muslim population.

The arrival in Baku about this time of a German mission from Astrakhan to discuss the supply of oil, cotton and manganese and the repatriation of prisoners of war added to the hostility of the new Baku government towards the Bolsheviks. The suspicion of Soviet acceptance of German demands for deliveries of raw materials, including oil and cotton, was confirmed by the arrival of the German mission which had travelled with every facility placed at its disposal through Russia to the Caspian port of Astrakhan.

The mission, which was evidently unaware of the turn of events or the presence of the British, was interned. This incident, and the information being received from Tiflis and London regarding negotiations between Berlin and Moscow for the supply of oil to Germany, provided conclusive evidence in British eyes that the Soviet government was in no position to resist German demands, and thus, in effect, was party to the latter's plans to secure shipments of oil, manganese, cotton and other supplies from the Caucasus and Turkistan. This in itself, it was felt, fully justified the British step in providing assistance to the Baku government in defending Baku against Turko-German seizure.[5]

German and Turkish aims were now clearly in conflict in the Caucasus, and the Bolsheviks were endeavouring to take advantage of this situation. By assenting to German demands, the Soviet government in Moscow sought to persuade Berlin to put pressure on the Turkish government and military command to halt the attack on Baku, the main source of oil supplies. With this end in view, the Bolsheviks had entered into an agreement with the German government for the provision of supplies in addition to those which were included in the terms of the Brest-Litovsk Treaty. This supplementary agreement, which was negotiated by the Soviet plenipotentiary in Berlin, Joffe, and signed on August 27th, had become known to the Turkish Command, which thereupon decided to hasten the advance to the Caspian.

As one of Dunsterville's aims was to prevent supplies of oil reaching the enemy, the hostility towards him displayed by the Soviet's representatives in Baku was understandable. The intervention of the British force in Baku on the invitation of the local government was (and still is) represented as 'imperialism', whereas the German advance into the Caucasus was glossed over as a breach of the terms of the Brest-Litovsk Treaty.[6]

On his arrival in Baku on August 17th with reinforcements consisting of a small detachment of the Hampshire and North Staffordshire regiments and several armoured cars, Dunsterville at once entered into negotiations with the Centro-Caspian government for the substitution of the existing division of military command for a single command, and for the provision of supplies. His efforts in that direction, however, were unavailing. The Baku government evidently looked to him to provide not only military equipment but also troops in sufficient numbers to take over the main task of defending the city. The Centro-Caspian government was informed that Dunsterville's small force was in Baku to help in the organization of defence, to provide a limited amount of equipment and to assist in the training of the government's own troops, but not to undertake the whole task of defending the city. It was evident that the government had little faith in their own forces, and that the declarations of its members to fight to the last man were little more than empty rhetoric. Within a fortnight after the arrival of the British force in Baku it was evident that little reliance could be placed on the local troops or on the ability of the Centro-Caspian government to organize their own resources for defence. In addition to the military stores recaptured from the Soviet ships on the evacuation of Soviet military forces from Baku on August 12th, vast stocks of army equipment, including guns and ammunition, were discovered at different points in the city, unused and unguarded. Dunsterville took steps to have these assembled at a central point near the docks, and set up workshops to repair and assemble guns, vehicles and other equipment.

More than fifty guns, many of them new weapons that had been supplied by the Allies to the Russian government during the war, were
discovered, as well as a large quantity of shells and explosives.

There was no lack of equipment and ammunition for the defence
of the city; what was lacking was willingness to fight, and, in the case
of commanding officers, to subordinate themselves to a central and
unified command. The Armenians, who formed the major part of the
Baku troops, despite their fear of the Turks, showed no disposition to
fight, abandoning their position on the slightest sign of enemy movement. The 'Tartar' population was hostile to the Armenians, and waited
only for the entry of the Turks to slaughter and loot the properties of
their hated rivals. The government made promises to put their house
in order and build up an effective defence system, but it was obvious
that having obtained British co-operation, they were content to leave
the fighting to the British and make them responsible for the outcome,
whether favourable or otherwise.

Such was the picture of the position in Baku at the end of August.
The fall of Baku seemed to be imminent, and the fate of General
Dunsterville's 900 troops uncertain, despite steps taken to hold ships
in readiness for evacuation. With less than this number of troops in
Enzeli and along the line of communication with Kazvin and Bagdad,
and only one battalion of infantry and three squadrons of cavalry at
Malleson's disposal, continued resistance to a determined enemy
advance eastward towards India would seem to depend mainly on
naval control of the Caspian, fortification of the ports of Krasnovodsk
and Enzeli, and some measure of British control over the western
sector of the Central Asian railway.

Failing an early enemy defeat on the Western front, or a separate
Turkish collapse, which at that time seemed unlikely, there now
appeared to be little hope of holding Baku. Effective Soviet resistance
to German and Turkish military plans in the Caucasus and Central
Asia was unlikely in view of the breakaway of the three Transcaucasian
peoples from Russian control, the confused state of affairs in Turkistan
and the recently concluded arrangements for supply of oil and other
raw materials to Germany. Soviet leaders seemed at that time to be
more concerned with consolidating their own power and putting into
force their social and revolutionary theories, whether these conformed

to the aspirations of the Russian people or not, than in resisting German and Turkish demands.

Faced with counter-revolution in south Russia, the north Caucasus and Siberia, the Soviet government's hands were too firmly tied by the terms of the Brest-Litovsk Treaty and the supplementary agreements to do more than offer token resistance without outside help. British help in the Caucasus was rejected as having imperialist aims, and more violent hostility was being displayed towards Russia's former allies than towards the German and Turkish invaders.

4

Agreement with Ashkhabad

THE negotiations between the Ashkhabad government and General Malleson were conducted in Meshed, on behalf of the former, by Vladimir Dokhov, representing Zimen, the Minister for External Affairs, and in Ashkhabad by Captain Teague-Jones, who on General Malleson's behalf dealt directly with Zimen. As Dokhov, although fully authorized, did not inspire complete confidence, it was thought desirable to maintain direct liaison with Zimen, so that knotty points could be resolved without delay, but also to be assured from Teague-Jones's personal contacts and from his observation on the spot that the Committee was in a position to implement any undertakings they might assume. Teague-Jones, who spoke fluent Russian, as well as several Eastern languages, and had had a wide experience on the North-West Frontier of India and in Persia, had already made himself familiar with the situation in Baku and Transcaspia, and had a keen appreciation of the seriousness of the impending threat to Baku and Central Asia generally. The possibilities presented by co-operation with the Transcaspian government of checking that threat, and of denying to the enemy access to the oil and cotton he so ardently sought, did not blind Teague-Jones to the inherent weakness of the Transcaspian regime, the inexperience of its members and the internal difficulties with which it inevitably would be beset. His advice was therefore of the greatest value to General Malleson and enabled the General, in his dealings with Dokhov, to keep the negotiations on a realistic basis.

Dokhov was a typical example of the Russian worker-revolutionary. Full of partially digested theory, he combined a supreme confidence in his own knowledge and capacity with an extremely limited understanding of the outside world. Like many Russians of peasant origin, he was suspicious and cunning, although not lacking intelligence. In a destructive phase of the revolution he showed some constructive ability, or at least seemed to grasp the idea that the smashing of idols and slaughter of opponents were not ends in themselves, as so many revolutionary leaders appeared to think at that time.

The Transcaspian government, in desperate straits, was chiefly concerned in obtaining help in the form of supplies, equipment and money. Conscious of its weakness in manpower, it sought assistance from the British from necessity rather than from any fraternal desire to welcome their presence. Although fully aware of the Turko-German threat, the Transcaspians, not unnaturally, were less concerned with it than with their own immediate needs. Their willingness to co-operate with the British in measures to contain that threat and, if necessary, to block enemy progress from across the Caspian, derived from the desperate situation in which they found themselves since their break with Tashkent.

In Baku, as we have seen, Dunsterville was finding little inclination on the part of the local politicians and national leaders to sink their internal differences and organize resistance to the Turks, or to put the oil and harbour installations out of action. Malleson, faced with the possibility of a similar situation arising at Krasnovodsk and along the Central Asian railway, now made it known to the Executive Committee at Ashkhabad that he was not prepared to leave these and other defensive measures to chance or to expressions of goodwill by the local authorities, and therefore insisted that the British Mission be given some measure of control over the working of the railway and the port of Krasnovodsk during the period of hostilities.[1]

This stipulation, accepted by the Ashkhabad Committee, no doubt contributed to the suspicion, subsequently to be presented in Soviet journalism and official histories as a 'fact', that British aims were to establish themselves in Turkistan permanently.

The need to reconcile the aims and needs of both parties gave rise to hard bargaining, but the pressure of events brought about agreement. The approval of Simla and London to the agreement had to be obtained. A draft of the 'protocol' or proposed text of the formal agreement was submitted to London and to headquarters in India, and was supported by an urgent plea by Malleson for authority to confirm the arrangement and provide the necessary equipment required by Ashkhabad. After some delay Malleson's proposals were accepted, but evidently with some hesitation, the authorities in London being in some doubts as to the desirability of British troops being involved in operations in Transcaspia.[2]

Although no formal agreement was ever signed between the two parties, the 'protocol' was initialled on August 19th and immediately came into operation.

In the introduction to the agreement both parties expressed their aims as follows:

(a) The establishment of peace and order in Transcaspia and Russian Turkistan.

(b) Agreement to resist Turko-German plans to seize and exercise political authority in Transcaspia and Turkistan.

In the characteristic parlance of official diplomatic documents the Transcaspian Committee declared that it sought British assurance that Baku, as the 'key to Russian Central Asia', would be defended, and that British troops and guns would be made available for the defence of Krasnovodsk against a Bolshevik or Turko-German attack. On the British side an undertaking was given that Baku would be defended against the advancing Turks, and that steps would be taken to ensure a supply of oil and petrol to Krasnovodsk; also that measures would be undertaken to put Krasnovodsk into a state of defence against enemy attack from the sea.

For their part the Transcaspian government undertook to place at the disposal of the British for this purpose steamers and other vessels in its possession; to grant use of the port of Krasnovodsk and provide assistance in building up its defences; and, in the event of necessity, to withdraw all rolling stock from the port, destroy all oil and water tanks along the railway, and render the railway unusable by the enemy by wrecking bridges, telegraphs and lines. The government also undertook to withhold the export of cotton during the period of hostilities.

For its immediate needs the Transcaspian government sought and the British Mission agreed to the provision of 1,000 rifles with ammunition, machine-guns, Mauser ammunition, explosives for use against bridges, etc., instructors in the use of these weapons and supplies and the training, at Meshed, of a Transcaspian machine-gun section. In addition, the agreement provided for the participation by British troops, at mutually agreed points, in operations along the railway; it being understood that, owing to the difficulties of supply and the length of the line of communications with India, large numbers could not be expected.

The Transcaspian government also undertook to provide the British with facilities in the use of railways, telegraphic and radio communications, and for the supply of provisions for their troops; to accept liaison officers at the front; and to repair the road between Meshed and the Persian frontier.

In response to the Transcaspian government's request for financial assistance, it was agreed on the British side that financial help would be granted 'for the fulfilment of these aims', the sum and method to be the subject of further discussion. It was also agreed that the expenditure of any subsidy that might be provided would be subject to joint control.

On the subject of Command it was agreed that any British troops that might be made available for service on the front facing Tashkent would come under the command of the Transcaspian 'High Command', but that any orders issued to them would be transmitted through British liaison officers. However, British troops stationed for specific defence purposes at Krasnovodsk would not be moved except with British agreement.[3]

It will be seen from the above that the agreement, in certain points, had something of a provisional character. However, regarding measures to resist or impede the Turkish advance, the Transcaspian government gave definite assurances that it would take certain precautionary steps with British supervision for the defence of Krasnovodsk. Its further needs for military material were noted, and steps were taken by a Malleson to satisfy them to the best of his ability.

The agreement was necessarily indefinite concerning finance and the availability of troops, as there was no certainty on the British side that additional troops would be placed at General Malleson's disposal. Final agreement with Ashkhabad on the provision of funds would also depend on his own assessment of the Committee's needs and of its capacity to make proper use of any financial assistance that might be made available. Moreover, the difficulties of exchange and currency would have to be surmounted, as more than one currency was in use, with varying and unpredictable rates of exchange.

It cannot be said that the Transcaspian government was wholly satisfied with the terms of this agreement, which committed them to actions in which a large section of the population seemed to have little

44

interest, and which, in the eyes of some of them at least, infringed their sovereignty. Members of the government, however, publicly expressed themselves as satisfied and, in the Press, emphasis was placed on the military and financial help that was forthcoming and the steps that were to be taken with British financial assistance to overcome the economic crisis, raise wages and relieve the public lot generally.

In anticipation of the signing of the agreement, preliminary steps had been taken by the Mission to speed up supplies. Troops were beginning to arrive in Meshed from Birjand and Seistan; a transport park was set up, and motor vehicles, many of them in need of reconditioning after their long journeys over the still only partly reconstructed road, were gradually replacing camel transport for the delivery of urgently needed equipment and stores.[4]

By the end of August preparations to reinforce the detachment of the 19th Punjabis in Transcaspia were in full swing. Disillusioned with the faded charms of east Persia, even the more hard-bitten officers and men were elated with the prospect of action in the land beyond the Hindu Kush, a region that had stirred the imagination of the British army in India for the past fifty years. Beyond the border lay Bukhara, Samarkand, Khiva—legendary cities that had attracted nineteenth-century explorers like Wolff and Vambery, and the two unfortunate British officers, Conolly and Stoddart, who had been murdered by the Emir of Bukhara in 1842. Although it was realized that these fabulous places were far beyond the probable scene of action, their propinquity stirred the imagination. Most frontier officers of the Indian army had read Kipling's *Kim*, or had observed the Uzbek and Bukharan traders who came down to the bazaars of Peshawar through the Khyber Pass with their rugs, silks and lambskins. The two Indian regiments under Malleson's command were familiar with frontier duties, and were to acquit themselves well in the operations to follow, and add to the honourable traditions of the Indian army.

The Malleson Mission was now committed to support of the Transcaspians in resisting attack from Tashkent. For its part, the Transcaspians had undertaken to place the railway and the port of Krasnovodsk at the disposal of the British in the event of a Turkish advance across the Caspian. Arrangements were quickly made for the exchange of liaison officers, and for communications, and by arrangement with Dunsterville for some reinforcement by a small detachment of British troops from Enzeli to join the British-Indian detachments already in Transcaspia.

The terms of this agreement with Ashkhabad, and the circumstances in which it was concluded, have been misrepresented in Soviet and many other accounts (based on Soviet reports) of events in Central Asia in 1918 and 1919. It may therefore be appropriate at this point to recapitulate briefly the particular circumstances that prevailed at that time.

Despite the conclusion of the Peace Treaty signed at Brest-Litovsk, the Germans and Turks had continued to advance into Russian territory, to seize raw materials to enable them to prosecute the war against the Allies and extend their operations into Persia, Afghanistan and Central Asia and to threaten India.

Animosity directed against the Allied Powers, and particularly the British, was being whipped up by Soviet propaganda and intrigue, and anti-British agitators were being given sanctuary by Moscow and Tashkent and provided with funds and facilities to conduct their activities. While denying the right of national minorities in Turkistan (despite fair promises made to them to accord them freedom to manage their own affairs) to participate in local government and administration, the Soviet government and its Turkistan offshoot directed charges of 'colonialism' and 'imperialism' in Asia against Allied governments, while continuing the former Tsarist policy of repression and exclusion against the Muslim population of Turkistan.[5]

In these circumstances the authorities in India were obliged to take defensive action. Turkish and German penetration of Persia was increasing in scope. In view of the growing Turkish military threat to north Persia, the British Command at Bagdad had no alternative but to improvise means to fill the gap in the defence positions in Persia created by the withdrawal of Russian troops. That these steps would be suspect in Soviet eyes was to be expected, but that they would be regarded in Moscow with greater hostility than German and Turkish penetration of the Caucasus and other Russian territory was a lesson that had yet to be learnt.

Bolshevik radio propaganda, which had now reached a shrill note (the Murmansk landing having taken place, and opposition to the

Soviet regime developing in Siberia, the Caucasus, Turkistan and else-where), was now accusing the British of acting with the connivance of American 'capitalism' in accordance with a specific plan to seize and colonize Russian Central Asia. It may well be that the Soviet govern-ment, like the Tsarist regime, suspicious of British policies in that part of the world, and obsessed with the characteristic Russian search for a motive behind every action, at that time did really believe in the existence of such a plan. But to members of the Mission, and to those in command of British forces in Persia, only too well aware of the vacillations of their own authorities in Whitehall, and at Bagdad and Simla, and of official reluctance to accept the recommendations of the two generals in the field of operations, there was no sign of any plan, territorial or otherwise, in the often vague and cautious communica-tions that they were receiving from their headquarters in London and India.

Despite all evidence of the hastily improvised character and limited scope of British operations in north-east Persia and in the Caspian area, it is invariably stated in Soviet accounts of these operations that they formed part of an overall plan to seize and subjugate Russian Turkistan. The Ashkhabad revolt in July 1918 continues to be repre-sented as having been instigated by the Malleson Mission, whereas the Mission had not arrived in Meshed at that time. Dunsterville is equally charged with having brought about the replacement of the Baku Soviet by the Centro-Caspian government. These Soviet accusations are in keeping with the official Soviet version of domestic events throughout Turkistan in 1918 and 1919, in which it is alleged British and American intrigue played an active part. The then American Vice-Consul in Tashkent, Roger G. Tredwell, is accused of having aided and abetted 'White' Russian forces, and of having supported (in collab-oration with the British) 'White' Russian counter-revolutionary activity in Tashkent. The 'Basmachi' revolt of the Muslim population in Turkistan which followed the Tashkent Soviet's suppression of an attempt to create an autonomous government at Kokand, and the splits and betrayals within the Tashkent Bolshevik's own ranks, are indiscriminately attributed to British and American machinations. (The part played by Americans in these activities is never clearly defined, but is usually referred to the influence of Wall Street!) In fact, all these events stemmed from local causes, chiefly from the chauvinism and short-sighted policies of the Russian-dominated Soviet in Tashkent in excluding all but their own Russian party members from the government and administration.

It was not until Moscow intervened in the autumn of 1919 by sending the so-called 'Turkistan Commission' to Tashkent that steps were taken to pacify the Muslim population and win their support for the Soviet regime.

Several years were to elapse before pacification of the region was achieved by a combination of military strength and promises of internal reforms, which, however, were to prove illusory to those Turkistanis who laid down their arms in the hope of achieving some measure of autonomy and self-government by negotiation. Union of the various racial groups was precluded by division of Turkistan into five separate regional republics, nominally autonomous, but controlled by the centre at Moscow. The form of autonomy was conceded, but the substance was lacking, and all attempts by Turkistani leaders, whether in the service of the state or not, to place national interests first, were destined to be mercilessly crushed.

5

Tashkent Attacks

HAVING extricated his badly mauled forces from Dushakh, Oraz Sirdar had taken up a position at Kaakha, a station ninety miles east of Ashkhabad. The village, a small one, was surrounded by walled gardens, irrigated from a stream which crossed the railway about a mile to the east of the station buildings. The position occupied by the Transcaspians in and to the left of the station was dominated by a hill north-east of the village, to the south of which the railway circled before continuing eastwards to the Bolshevik position nine miles away.

Reports received in Meshed from liaison officers and from the commander of the machine-gun section at Artyk indicated that the morale of the Ashkhabad troops was low, and that in numbers and equipment, particularly artillery, they were far inferior to the enemy. The total force at Oraz Sirdar's disposal consisted of about 1,000 infantry, of which not more than 100 were ex-soldiers of the old Russian army; the rest being only partially trained Russian and Armenian workers, a few Turkman infantry, a company of railway engineers and about 800 Turkman horsemen. The only artillery, apart from two 16-pounders mounted on an armoured train, was a battery of four light field guns and three muzzle-loaders, all served by ex-officers.

A second armoured train, which also carried water-butts and stores, provided accommodation for troops and was used by them for sleeping quarters. Chastened by events at Bairam Ali, the train-crews kept their trains in readiness to move at a moment's notice, a situation that was not conducive to any serious attempt to construct a defensive position on the flanks of the railway line.

The Turkman cavalry had so far proved to be of little military value. Undisciplined and independent, they came and went as they thought fit, and could not be relied upon to carry out any orders in an operation where their protective role on the flanks of a defensive position would

D

be an essential factor. Ready enough to cut up stragglers, and addicted to looting, their only use was in reconnaissance or in following up an enemy retreat. So far there had been little opportunity to use them in either capacity.

The Bolshevik force, superior in numbers and equipment, was provided with several 4·5 guns from the Kushkh arsenal. Austro-Hungarian ex-prisoners in its ranks had been told that the only obstacle to freedom and repatriation was the 'White guard' rebel force on the railway between Chardzhou and Krasnovodsk, and that, on reaching the Caspian, arrangements would be made for their return to their homelands.

The armoured trains on the enemy side were heavier and equipped with artillery of longer range than those possessed by the Transcaspians. This gave them a distinct advantage over the Transcaspians, who were obliged to keep at a safe distance from their opponents. Except for long-range shelling, and defensive action, trains were of little use to the enemy in offensive action in the early stage, as sections of the railway line were removed ahead of the position to prevent use being made of a 'runaway' locomotive.

Intelligence reports, now coming in from Sarakhs, Tedzhen and Merv, where all messages passing through the telegraph office were being tapped, showed that considerable reinforcement of the Bolsheviks was in progress. In spite of the demand on their resources for the operations against Dutov near Orenburg, and the native Muslim revolts against their rule throughout Turkistan, the Tashkent Bolsheviks had succeeded in mobilizing a fairly large force, and was now making extensive use of the 35,000 Austro-Hungarian and German prisoners of war who had been incarcerated in camps near Samarkand and Tashkent. Their most serious shortage was fuel, and they were greatly hampered by the near famine conditions that prevailed throughout the countryside.[1]

On the morning of August 24th the Bolsheviks moved up one armoured train and shelled the Transcaspian position at Kaakha for a short period without doing much damage. This was followed by cavalry reconnaissance action, enemy patrols on both flanks and on the high ground east of Kaakha penetrating within rifle shot of the station. After a certain amount of rifle and machine-gun fire by each side the Bolsheviks retired to their main position, and no further action took place on that day.

The morale of the Transcaspians, still low after the series of reverses suffered in the retreat from Repetek, rose a little after this engagement. The inability of their artillery to outrange the Bolshevik guns confined their use to defence, a difficult task in view of the nature of the country and the lack of protection on the flanks of the position.

Both sides lived in trains, and in the case of the Transcaspians the experience of the past month induced the rank-and-file to place more reliance on the mobility of the trains than on defensive positions. The limited range of the guns on the armoured train disposed the troops to remain in its vicinity, so that their freedom of action was determined by their means of retreat.

One company of the 19th Punjabis and a machine-gun section arrived at Kaakha from Artyk on the evening of the 25th. Its commander immediately made a reconnaissance of the defences and the disposition of the Transcaspian forces, which at first glance seemed to be placed to facilitate a quick retreat rather than to resist an enemy attack in force. Apart from a small body of Turkmans who had taken up a position in an old fort on a small hill about a mile to the north-east of the railway station, the high ground east of the main position was unoccupied. The main body of troops was concentrated in and around the station or in the orchards and gardens in its vicinity. An advanced post with one machine-gun was at the bridge a few hundred yards east of the station, and the three field guns were in position behind a low ridge south of the station. The muzzle-loaders, more dangerous to the gunners who operated them than to the enemy, were behind the northern extension of the same ridge, on the left of the railway.

The left flank was thus almost completely exposed, while failure to occupy the high ground east of the station made the main position particularly vulnerable.

On the arrival of the second and third companies of the 19th Punjabis later in the day, Lieutenant-Colonel Knollys, in command of the regiment, took part in a conference with the Transcaspian commander Colonel Oraz Sirdar and his staff. It was evident that Oraz Sirdar had little confidence that his troops would be able to hold the position in the event of a resolute attack, and that the dispositions made by his officers were little more than precautionary. The arrival of the Indian troops, and the promise of further reinforcements, including several guns which were on their way from Krasnovodsk, did something

51

towards raising morale, and Colonel Knollys's suggestions for some modification of the existing arrangements were readily accepted. Before any major changes could be put into effect, however, news of an impending enemy advance from Arman Sagat began to come in. During the night of the 25th one company of the Punjabis and a machine-gun section were posted on the exposed left flank, the remainder being held in reserve near the railway station where they could be quickly despatched to reinforce a counter-attack on either flank or assist in holding up an attempt to seize the station.

At about 7 a.m. on the 26th the 'Red' forces, which had occupied the high ground east of Kaakha, began to shell the Transcaspian lines with its forward batteries, but as their fire was very inaccurate, little damage was done and casualties were light. Some 'Red' infantry advanced down the hill and directed sporadic fire into the Transcaspian lines, but were driven off by machine-gun fire and the noise, if not the missiles, of the ancient muzzle-loaders.

The expected turning movement against the Transcaspian left flank began at 8 a.m. covered by rifle fire from the high ground and a certain amount of artillery fire. The fort occupied by the Turkman cavalry proved to be no obstacle to the advance, the Turkman troops scattering in disorder without making any serious attempt to defend it. The enemy advance into the cultivated ground north of the station, although slowed down by the rifle and machine-gun fire of the Punjabis, continued, and by 11 a.m. an attack on the station developed.

The Transcaspian infantry had fallen back on the trains, and for a moment it looked as though the position was lost. The reserve company of the Punjabis came up at this time, charging the enemy with fixed bayonets. Completely taken by surprise at this unexpected resistance, and to a form of warfare to which they were evidently unaccustomed, the 'Reds' fell back in disorder, and a running fight through the orchards and gardens continued for some time, and was rather belatedly joined by some of the Transcaspian troops who had retired to the shelter of the trains.

At close quarters it was difficult to distinguish friend from enemy, the Russian and Hungarian troops on the Bolshevik side being attired in the same nondescript uniforms as the troops of the Transcaspian force. This caused considerable confusion, and doubtless casualties on both sides were incurred through mistaken identity.

A street scene

The British Consulate

MESHED

The Maidan

Annenkovo: The front line

The author at Ashkhabad

Annenkovo: 28th Indian cavalry officers

At one point during the retirement the enemy made an attempt to hold a parley, but, while this was under discussion, rifle fire recommenced from the direction of the hill and fighting continued. The enemy then began to retire in disorder, leaving several machine-guns and a quantity of ammunition. By the early evening they had disappeared into the desert, and, except for some fire from one of their armoured trains, no further action took place until early in September.

There can be little doubt that the action of the Punjabis saved the situation. The Russian gunners, mainly ex-officers, and some of the Transcaspian infantry, behaved admirably, but the main body of the Transcaspian force, consisting chiefly of Armenians, showed little fight. Staff work was poor, none of Oraz Sirdar's aides displaying any initiative or intelligent appreciation of tactics, or of the use of natural features.

On the credit side, medical arrangements were good, nursing orderlies and even nurses from Ashkhabad hospitals appearing on the scene during the course of the action and displaying more courage than many of the troops.

Casualties on both sides were fairly high, considering the numbers engaged; proportionately the British-Indian force suffered a high percentage, having lost three officers killed and wounded (including the two liaison officers, both wounded) and twenty-four rank-and-file killed and wounded. The Transcaspians lost between thirty and forty, mainly wounded, while the enemy's losses were estimated to be at least three times that number, a considerable proportion of these having been incurred during the counter-attack on the station and orchards.

On the morning following the engagement a reinforcement, in the shape of a company of the 1/4 Hampshire Regiment, arrived from Enzeli via Krasnovodsk. The expected guns, a battery of the 44th Royal Field Artillery, followed a few days later.[2]

The engagement at Kaakha made it clear that the British contingent would have to rely on its own initiative in future action. This would necessitate the exercise of much tact in relations with the Transcaspian Command, particularly as Colonel Oraz Sirdar was being subjected to continual interference by his own government and by the rule of committees. The indiscipline of the Turkman troops and their unreliability in action ruled them out as a factor in defensive planning, while the latent suspicion between proletarian and non-proletarian at

Ashkhabad and elsewhere militated against efficiency in government and administration.

Oraz Sirdar and his staff, however, showed a disposition to lean on the British commander for advice, and made no serious difficulties when the latter, concerned for the safety and proper use of his own officers and men, made his own decisions. The government, weak and divided as it was to be, and inexperienced in public affairs, was becoming dependent on the army for its own continuance in office, as the loss of the Merv oasis had deprived it of its chief source of foodstuffs. Unless Merv, or at least Tedzhen, could be regained before the winter, famine would intervene, in which case popular support for the government would inevitably be withdrawn.

These questions were discussed in Ashkhabad in a conference which followed the Kaakha battle. The Askhabad government, with the promise of British support to sustain them, called for an immediate advance and the early reoccupation of Merv; the Army Command in return demanded reforms and improved arrangements for supply. The British stood by their undertakings, and promised to speed up the arrival of the cavalry force from Meshed and guns from Krasnovodsk, but at the same time urged certain changes in staff organization and personnel, both at the front and in the rear.

After some discussion agreement was reached to put into effect the changes demanded, and the Transcaspian Army Commander undertook to prepare for an advance as soon as reinforcements became available, supply and equipment needs satisfied, and, above all, the artillery position improved.

To add to other difficulties at the front, sickness was taking a heavy toll of the Transcaspian force. This was partly due to the insanitary conditions on the trains and at the front line, the extreme heat and lack of water. Influenza was also rife, many men of the Indian regiment being temporarily out of action with this complaint.

The rigour of the Turkistan climate was to prove a severe test of our men's endurance. Even the Indian troops, accustomed to the high temperatures of the Indian plains, found the dust and heat of the Central Asian desert extremely trying. In summer the temperature at midday rose to more than 120°F., falling steeply at night. In winter temperatures below zero were common, while high winds, both in summer and winter, raged across the desert, carrying dust in summer and sharp gritty snow in winter as additional discomforts.

Following the battle of Kaakha and the subsequent talks at Ashkhabad, the Kaakha position was reorganized. The line was extended well out into the flanks, and advance posts were established along the ridge and on the hill to the east. The main position on the left flank was taken over by the Punjabis, while detachments from the same regiment were posted on the ridge and at the bridgehead; the remainder of the Punjabis were kept in reserve with the Hampshires. Barbed wire, brought up from Meshed in Persian *fourgons* (large springless carts), was extensively used to strengthen the trenchworks and the gun positions, shortly to be increased in number with the arrival of the battery from Krasnovodsk.

By arrangement with General Malleson, some fifty selected men, mainly Russians, were sent from Ashkhabad to Meshed, there to be trained in the use of Vickers machine-guns. Equipment for this unit was found by the Meshed Mission, which also undertook the cost of maintenance and supply while they were in Persia.

Reinforcement by the 28th Cavalry Regiment, which had been in Meshed for several weeks, was speeded up. Rifles, ammunition and explosives were beginning to arrive from India, and their further transport to Ashkhabad was put in hand without delay.

Meanwhile a critical situation had developed at Baku, where General Dunsterville's troops were now fully engaged, preventing any additional troops and equipment being made available to Malleson from that quarter for any purpose other than the fortification of Krasnovodsk. Steps had been taken by General Malleson's officers to ensure that the undertaking of the Ashkhabad government to immobilize the railway and port installations in any emergency would be carried out. A mobile railway and mining unit was formed by the Transcaspian command, and arrangements were made by Malleson with Dunsterville for Engineers from Enzeli to be transported to Krasnovodsk in the event of the fall of Baku.

The Ashkhabad government had in the meantime been strengthened by the appointment of General Kruten as 'Defence Adviser', and the appointment of additional Ministers. These changes, while enhancing the capacity of the government to carry out its functions, somewhat altered its political constitution, and were to play a part in the crisis in its internal affairs which was to develop towards the end of the year.

As was to be expected, changes in command and in the organization of its forces were also made by the Tashkent government after the defeat at Kaakha. A whole series of decrees issued by the Revolutionary Military Soviet, dealing with mobilization of men and resources, agitation among the Moslem population and the tightening up of controls, became known to British Intelligence officers almost as soon as they were promulgated, and information received from points behind the front indicated clearly that a further attack, on a much heavier scale, must shortly be expected.

Before going on to the story of these operations, however, it is essential to return to the position at Baku. The presence of British and Indian troops in Transcaspia was mainly due to the Turko-German threat to Persia and India. That threat now seemed more immediate, and the danger existed that the small Anglo-Indian force might find itself too heavily involved in purely Transcaspian affairs at a time when all available resources might be needed to stem the threat from the Caucasus.

6

The Fall of Baku and the Twenty-six Commissars

THE first news received in Ashkhabad and Meshed of the fall of Baku came from a Turkish wireless message intercepted on September 15th. No official intimation of the disaster was received by the Malleson Mission until the morning of the 16th. The news was not unexpected, as it was known that Dunsterville had lost confidence in the ability of the Centro-Caspian government to organize defence or inspire its troops to fight. He had already taken steps to hold ships ready to evacuate his force, but in the chaotic conditions that prevailed it seemed far from certain that he would be able to get them away.

On the 17th news was received by the Mission at Meshed that Dunsterville had arrived back at Enzeli with his troops, and that he had succeeded in evacuating his sick and wounded and a considerable quantity of military equipment. The story of the evacuation, at night and under fire not only from Turkish guns but also from Baku guard-ships, is an epic which General Dunsterville has described with dramatic force in his book *The Adventures of Dunsterforce*.

As the mixed local force of Baku defenders fell back on the city in face of the Turkish onslaught, abandoning positions with little attempt to defend them, rearguard action was left to the British infantry, which held out until the main body of the British had withdrawn through the town to the dock area.[1]

Shelling was heavy, taking its toll of casualties among the civilian population, especially in the Armenian quarter, which had evidently been chosen as a target by the Turkish gunners. The Azerbaijani mob, organized by Turkish agents, was already on the prowl, killing Armenians and looting their houses.

The Centro-Caspian government had collapsed, and all semblance of public order was at an end by nightfall. In the dock area British troops held key points, holding several ships with steam up to evacuate sick and wounded.

As it became clear that no further resistance was to be expected from government forces, Dunsterville decided to evacuate the whole of his force.

As night fell, all British troops were withdrawn to the docks. Despite a threat by the commander of a government gunboat to prevent the departure of the British, several ships, with the whole of the British force, including its sick and wounded, crept out of the harbour in the darkness, while the crash of bursting shells reverberated among the rooftops of the stricken city.

A considerable quantity of artillery and ammunition had been evacuated with the troops. By agreement with Malleson part of this equipment was later sent to Krasnovodsk with a small detachment of artillerymen and naval personnel to help build up the defences of that port against a possible Turkish attack.

By withdrawing the best of the Caspian ships, several of which had been armed as auxiliary cruisers, Dunsterville sought to keep control of the southern waters of the Caspian, while at the same time depriving the enemy of the means of transporting large numbers of troops and military equipment to Krasnovodsk.

The fall of Baku, although not unexpected, aroused the Ashkhabad Committee to a sense of the danger to which it was now exposed from two sides. As so often happened when Allied forces intervened during the civil war period, there was a tendency on the part of the local authority to sit back and leave the brunt of the fray to Allied troops.

In Meshed, where General Malleson's headquarters staff was still located, news of the withdrawal of Dunsterville's troops brought with it recognition of the dangerous position of the small mixed force strung along the length of the Central Asian railway.

Messages received from liaison officers at Ashkhabad were indicative of the state of near panic in Transcaspian circles. Plots against their own security were suspected, and drastic action against suspects was already taking place.

On the morning of September 18th the Ashkhabad Committee's liaison officer of Meshed, Dokhov, called on the Mission in a state of great excitement. He announced that he had received a telegram from

Ashkhabad on a matter of great importance and urgency, and that he had been instructed to communicate its contents to General Malleson and ask for his comments and advice.

Without producing the actual telegram, Dokhov informed General Malleson, in the presence of two of the General's staff officers, that a party of Bolshevik Commissars, former members of the Baku government that had been replaced by the Centro-Caspian Directorate at the end of July, had arrived at Krasnovodsk on the steamship *Turkman* and were being held under arrest by the Krasnovodsk Town Commandant, Kuhn. The Commissars, about thirty in number and including Shaumian, the former head of the Baku government, Korganov, Fioletov, Petrov and other prominent Bolsheviks, had been imprisoned by the Centro-Caspian authorities at the time of the evacuation of Soviet Russian forces to Astrakhan on August 14th, but had been released, or had escaped on the eve of the Turkish entry into Baku. According to Dokhov's account, the Commissars had left by sea that same evening, intending to go to Astrakhan, but for some reason, unknown to Dokhov, the ship had brought them to Krasnovodsk.[2]

Their presence in Krasnovodsk was a matter of great concern to the Ashkhabad Committee, the members of which were seriously alarmed that opposition elements in Transcaspia might take advantage of the presence of the Commissars to stage a revolt against the government. The chairman of the Committee therefore requested General Malleson to state his views as to what should be done.

Questioned by General Malleson, Dokhov was unable or unwilling to add very much to the message he had been instructed to convey. He admitted that his government was alarmed by the fall of Baku and was nervous about the revival of opposition to its authority in Ashkhabad, Krasnovodsk and elsewhere. They considered that the presence of the Commissars, even under arrest, constituted a danger, particularly at a time when the situation in the Caspian area was uncertain and the Merv area was still in Bolshevik hands.

General Malleson replied that he considered that in no circumstances should the Commissars be allowed to proceed along the railway to Ashkhabad. While it was a matter for the Committee to decide what steps they proposed to take to prevent this, he suggested that the best course would be for the Committee to hand the prisoners over to him to be held as hostages for British citizens imprisoned or held under restraint by the Soviet government. He saw some difficulty in determining a convenient point for the prisoners to be handed over, but thought this could be arranged.

Dokhov seemed to be dubious, but undertook to inform his government of General Malleson's suggestion, though adding the words: 'If it is not already too late.' Asked what he meant, Dokhov said his government might already have decided what steps to take. He then left.

Immediately afterwards General Malleson sent a telegram to his representative in Ashkhabad, Captain Teague-Jones, informing him what Dokhov had said and instructing him to get in touch with Zimen, the Foreign Minister, ascertain what the position was and telegraph a reply without delay. The General then telegraphed a summary of the conversation with Dokhov to his chiefs at Simla, notifying them of his suggestion that the Commissars be taken over by him and conveyed to India for internment as hostages and asking for instructions.

On the same evening Teague-Jones replied that he had been informed by Zimen of the arrival in Krasnovodsk of the Commissars and their arrest there. Zimen had undertaken to keep him informed and had said that the Committee was considering the matter that night. Teague-Jones added that Zimen was in a very nervous state but had given no indication of what the Committee had in mind.

As was subsequently ascertained, the Committee, consisting of Funtikov, Kurilov, Zimen and Dorrer, sat until a late hour that night, apparently without reaching an agreement. Teague-Jones endeavoured to keep in touch with Zimen, but when the latter, together with Dorrer, left the meeting after midnight Teague-Jones was told that the question had not yet been settled, and it was hinted that there was disagreement between the members as to the course to be taken. Teague-Jones also ascertained that Kuhn had been pressing for a decision, as he feared there might be a local insurrection to secure the release of the prisoners. Funtikov was in a semi-intoxicated state and suspicious of British motives in suggesting that the Commissars be held as hostages.

On the following morning Teague-Jones tried to get into touch with Zimen but without success. That evening he approached Funtikov personally, and found him still in a state of intoxication and not disposed to discuss the matter. Finally, when pressed, Funtikov admitted that it had been decided to shoot the prisoners, and that he had sent Kurilov to Krasnovodsk on the previous night to instruct Kuhn and

A wrecked armoured
train at Dushakh

Tekke Turkmans

Turkman troops
of the Transcaspian
government force

The Palace used as British staff headquarters

BAIRAM ALI

Turkman officers   Medical staff

make the necessary arrangements. He declined to discuss the matter any further.

Teague-Jones immediately informed Malleson, who sent for Dokhov. On presenting himself at the office of the Mission, Dokhov, who was in one of his taciturn moods, said in reply to Malleson's questions that he had 'just been notified that the prisoners have been shot; that the Committee has decided to take this action in view of the seriousness of the situation, and the difficulties involved in acceding to General Malleson's proposal'.

General Malleson's reply to this was that in his opinion they were 'all alike—Red or White'—and that Dokhov could inform his chiefs that he, Malleson, was 'horrified at the action taken'.

Dokhov, who was clearly shaken by Malleson's outburst, withdrew without any further comment. Neither at that time nor subsequently did he intimate that he had had any prior information about the Committee's intentions concerning the shooting of the prisoners.

Teague-Jones was thereupon instructed to pass to Zimen the same comment given to Dokhov. When he did so, Zimen, in a state of extreme agitation, stated that the decision was Funtikov's; that he (Zimen) and Dorrer were opposed to having the Commissars shot, and that Funtikov and Kurilov had taken matters into their own hands after the meeting and had given the order.

It transpired that on receipt of this order Kuhn had brought the Commissars, twenty-six in number, under guard from the prison late at night, indicating that they were being sent to Ashkhabad by order of the government authorities there. The train proceeded to a point some 200 kilometres east of Krasnovodsk, where it stopped. The prisoners were taken a short distance into the desert, and there, in the early morning of September 20th, were summarily shot. Exactly who carried out the shooting never became known, nor is it certain that any emissary of the Committee at Ashkhabad was present.

Every effort was made by the Ashkhabad Committee to keep the matter secret, and some time elapsed before rumours of what had happened reach the public. Members of the Committee, including those directly involved, began to show a disposition to dissociate themselves from Funtikov's views, and then and later sought a convenient scape-goat on whom responsibility for the shootings could be placed.

Several days after this episode took place, General Malleson was informed in reply to his telegram to Simla that they agreed with his suggestion that the Commissars be sent to India. Although it was already too late, the authorities in London, still unaware of what had happened, were considering the possibility of exchanging the Commissars, as well as other Bolsheviks who were in British hands, for British diplomats and officials who had been imprisoned by the Soviet government. At a later date, when the Soviet Foreign Commissar, M. Chicherin, sought information through neutral channels regarding the whereabouts of the Commissars, the Soviet government was informed that they were not and had never been in British hands.

Although anticipating the course of events it would be useful at this point to relate briefly what subsequently happened in relation to this affair. The fate of the Twenty-six Commissars did not become known in Moscow until early in the new year, or, if it was known, no public announcement was made. A short time after the reoccupation of Baku by British troops from Enzeli, following the Turkish capitulation, a Socialist-Revolutionary journalist, Vadim Chaikin by name, who had played some part in Soviet domestic affairs in Tashkent, and now evidently seeking to ingratiate himself with the Bolsheviks, visited Transcaspia from Baku, and there interviewed Funtikov in prison. On his return to Baku, then in British occupation after the Turkish withdrawal, he published an article in a local newspaper in which he accused the British of being responsible for the arrest and execution of the Twenty-six Commissars. He followed this up later with a book, published in Moscow, elaborating this theme, making the accusation that British officers were directly involved, and that the shooting had been carried out on British orders. He cited the 'confession' of former members of the Ashkhabad Committee, including Funtikov, as evidence.

Although Chaikin produced no factual evidence to substantiate his assertions, the Soviet government now publicly accused the British government of responsibility for the evacuation of the Commissars from Baku and for their subsequent arrest and execution. Statements contained in Chaikin's article and book were cited as 'evidence'. Reports of the shooting of the Commissars were broadcast by the Soviet Radio, while the Soviet Press was filled with articles describing how the Commissars were supposed to have met their end.[3]

Since that time the Soviet government has persisted in this charge,

Fig. 1. The shooting of the Twenty-six Commissars in September 1918, as depicted by the well-known artist I. I. Brodskiy (reproduced from *Istoriya Grazhdanskoy Voyny S.S.S.R.*, Moscow, 1957). Among the onlookers, the figures of two British officers are depicted. Evidently they are supposed to represent members of the Malleson Mission from Ashkhabad, which in Soviet accounts were allegedly present at the execution of the Commissars.

and has declined to accept any assurance from the British government that the facts are otherwise than as stated by Chaikin and other Soviet spokesmen at that time. The case of the Twenty-six Commissars now forms part of the epic story of the Soviet revolution. The version presented by Chaikin has become Soviet official history, so that it is included in the *Great Soviet Encyclopaedia* as a factual account of the episode, and paintings by Soviet artists and illustrations to books dealing with the civil-war period depict British officers as being present at the execution.

In fact no British officer was in the vicinity, nor was any British officer or official aware of what was happening to the prisoners until information was extracted from a drunken Funtikov after the event.[4]

The circumstances in which the Commissars were brought over from Baku have never been satisfactorily cleared up. It is uncertain whether the Centro-Caspian authorities ordered their release, or whether friends rescued them from prison during the chaos that prevailed on the eve of the Turkish occupation of the city. Various Soviet personalities claim to have effected their release, but there seems to be some mystery surrounding their departure on the *Turkman*. The captain of the vessel informed the authorities in Krasnovodsk that the ship was bound for Astrakhan when it left port, but that the crew declined to take it there, ostensibly because of fuel shortage. In all probability, some members of the crew were uncertain what fate held in store for them on their arrival in Astrakhan. In any case, the arrival of the ship was quite unexpected in Krasnovodsk, and it was only through the action of the guard-ship from which a message was sent ashore to Kuhn that the latter was able to apprehend the Commissars before they were able to land.

The full impact of this unhappy episode on relations between the Malleson Mission and the Ashkhabad Committee, and subsequently between the Soviet and British governments, was not to make itself felt for some time. Funtikov's action in disregarding Malleson's advice completely destroyed any reputation he may have enjoyed in the General's eyes. Malleson had no high regard for revolutionary leaders, whether Bolshevik, Menshevik or Socialist-Revolutionary. He considered them to be unprincipled demagogues, self-seeking leaders of the ignorant mob, all equally untrustworthy. If he had had any knowledge of the Russian language his attitude, forcibly expressed in public as well as in private, might well have added to the difficulties experienced by his Russian-speaking staff in their relations with members of the Committee and its representatives.

Meanwhile, direct communications had been established with Enzeli. General Dunsterville had returned to Bagdad shortly after the evacuation of his troops from Baku, and the command of the force, shortly to be renamed 'Norperforce', was taken over by Major-General Thompson. Captain Norris, R.N., who had been made available to General Dunsterville to organize naval units in the Caspian, made use of some of the retrieved artillery brought from Baku to arm several ships in case the Turks made an attempt to cross the Caspian to Krasnovodsk or tried to land troops in Persia. The detachment of infantry and gunners sent from Enzeli to Krasnovodsk early in October quickly took steps to strengthen the defences of the port.

During the next few weeks the inhabitants of Krasnovodsk waited anxiously to see what the Turks would do next, but in fact no Turkish move was made in that direction. It is uncertain whether they were deterred from making the attempt by lack of shipping or by the growing weakness of Turkish military strength. Conflict between the Turkish and German Commands may have played a part. After having consolidated their position in Baku, where many thousand unfortunate Armenians were massacred by the Azerbaijanis, the Turks moved part of their forces northward up the coast to Derbent in support of the Daghistanis who were in revolt against the Bolsheviks. Before Nuri Pasha had time to organize his forces for a more spectacular move the Turkish government sued for peace and the game was up.[5]

7

Malleson Acts

IN RETROSPECT it is not easy to see what the military authorities in Simla and London hoped might be achieved with the small British forces in north Persia in holding up the Turko-German advance. Although the Turks were known to be weakening, and that on some issues they were in conflict with the Germans, they had between 30,000 and 40,000 troops in the Caucasus, and two German divisions were already in Georgia or being rapidly formed there. The Bolsheviks, although occupied with counter-revolutionary and nationalist risings in the north Caucasus and Kuban, had a considerable naval and military force at Astrakhan, and were only awaiting the dislodgement of Ataman Dutov from Orenburg to pour 'Red' Army troops into Turkistan. The Austro-Hungarian and German war prisoners were potentially available to the enemy as reinforcements if the advance into Central Asia continued.[1]

Pan-Islamic propaganda, relatively ineffective elsewhere, mainly due to the successful Arab revolt against the Turks and the absence of any real unity of outlook in the Muslim world, was not without effect in Afghanistan and northern India and among the 'Ulema' and some native political leaders in Russian Turkistan. The Azerbaijanis were, for the most part, in collusion with Nuri Pasha's 'Army of Islam' and had facilitated its eastward advance, while in Transcaspia some Turkman leaders were known to be placing their hopes on Turkish help to regain their independence from the Russians, lost after a sanguinary struggle in the eighties of the last century.

In Meshed, at that time, the significance of the minor success at Kaakha was not overestimated. The strength and capacity of the Tashkent army had been tested, and it was the opinion of the commander of the Malmiss detachment in Transcaspia that with some reinforcement from Meshed and Krasnovodsk it would be possible to drive the Bolsheviks back beyond the Merv oasis and even to the Oxus, provided the attack could be made before the Tashkent Soviet government had obtained help from Russia and had completed the reorganization of its command. It was considered that this would help to stabilize the position of the Ashkhabad government and keep control of Krasnovodsk and the Central Asian railway between that port and the vital Merv–Tedzhen area in friendly hands. Occupation of Merv would also relieve the food shortage in Transcaspia, and would enable force to be brought to bear on the Kushkh outpost on the Afghan frontier, then in Bolshevik hands, from which point a road leads to Herat and via Farah to Kandahar and Quetta.

Although no promise of reinforcements was forthcoming from India, Malleson decided to proceed with his plan to provide additional support for the hard-pressed Ashkhabad government and strengthen Colonel Knollys's detachments. Orders were given to recruit additional local and Herati levies for lines of communications duties, while at the same time the Ashkhabad government was urged to try to win the confidence of the Turkman leaders by taking a prominent Turkman into the government. By this means it was hoped to encourage the Turkman leaders to provide a greater degree of support to the Transcaspian government.

Virtually isolated, and dependent on a line of communications 800 miles long, a thinly held mountain and desert track for supply and support, the position of Malmiss was even more precarious than that of the British base at Enzeli. Although the Enzeli base and line of communication was liable to be attacked by unfriendly Jangalis, and threatened from the direction of Tabriz, reinforcements could be sent to Enzeli from Bagdad by the Russian-made military road, whereas the Meshed–Quetta line of communications with long stretches of only partially constructed road was flanked by a potentially hostile Afghanistan and subjected to raids by tribesmen in the Seistan sector.

The speed with which work was being carried out along lines of communication between the railhead in Seistan and Meshed might have suggested to an intelligent enemy observer that preparations were on foot for the despatch of a considerable force to Meshed. In all probability, Turkish and German agents, as well as those employed by the Bolsheviks, reached this conclusion. But at the time the Malmiss Mission was despatched from India the possibility of a British military

67

force crossing the frontier into Transcaspia was not visualized. If this contingency had even been remotely considered by the chiefs of staff in Simla there was no sign that any provision had been made to deal with it. Apart from those troops already in operation as part of the East Persian Cordon force, and the locally recruited levies, no reinforcements were assembling at Quetta, nor did any additional troops arrive on the scene other than a few pioneers and signallers from Seistan and a small detachment from north-west Persia, sent at Malleson's request from Enzeli to Krasnovodsk at a later stage in the proceedings. Work on the road, and the establishment of supply depots, in a region where wheeled transport was hardly known, and supplies hard to obtain, served to meet the needs of the existing force but made little serious provision for contingencies that might arise should enemy forces succeed in crossing the Caspian.[2]

The East Persian Cordon Command, with its staff at Birjand, was now subordinate to General Malleson, and the appointment of an Inspector General of Communications, in the person of Brigadier-General W. E. Dickson, a capable and energetic officer with a flair for maintaining good relations with the local population and Persian officialdom, was to ensure that the flow of supplies along the long line would be maintained.

In these circumstances the most dangerous course was inaction. After consultation with the Transcaspian command plans were therefore put in hand to attack the Bolshevik line near Dushakh at the earliest possible moment and drive the 'Red' Army back beyond Merv. Colonel Knollys, commanding the British-Indian detachment, estimated that with the additional troops and artillery now promised from Enzeli, including the Russian machine-gun section that had been trained at Meshed, it should be possible to accomplish this by the end of September. It was known that the morale of the Red force had suffered as a result of the set-back at Kaakha, and that the performance of the Indian troops had struck terror in the hearts of the mixed collection of 'Red' Guard volunteers, ex-prisoners and conscripts that so far constituted the Tashkent army. Some weeks would elapse before the reorganization and reinforcement of the Bolsheviks could materially alter the situation. The engagement at Kaakha had almost ended in disaster for the Tashkent 'Red' Army and would undoubtedly have led their withdrawal beyond Merv if the Transcaspians had possessed reliable cavalry and had displayed some initiative in following up the retreat.

Preparations for the attack were interrupted but not seriously delayed by long-range shelling and probing operations carried out by the enemy on September 11th and 18th. While bringing up troop trains and reorganizing their forces, the Bolsheviks kept up reconnaissance with their cavalry, and on September 11th attempted a wide turning movement on the left flank which was easily repulsed. On the 18th a more determined turning movement by 'Red' cavalry, supported by heavy artillery fire from armoured trains, succeeded in reaching the railway in the rear of the Kaakha position, but was driven off by the Punjabi and 4th Hants reserves. The lack of reliable cavalry on the Transcaspian side hampered the defence in these operations. No reliance could be placed on the Turkman mounted troops, and it was not until the arrival of two squadrons of the 28th Cavalry on September 25th that this weakness was overcome.

By this time plans for the offensive were well advanced. The Transcaspian staff had been reorganized. A new chief of staff, Colonel Urusov, a regular staff officer, had been appointed, so that for the first time operational planning could be conducted on practical military lines. An aeroplane, so far lacking vital parts, had been made airworthy, and was brought up to the front for reconnaissance purposes. The armoured train was strengthened and provided with a heavier gun, and the fire power of the infantry had been improved by the provision of a number of Vickers machine-guns with trained crews.

The plan provided for an enveloping surprise attack on the enemy trains at Arman Sagad, the main attack to be made by a flank march to the north by infantry and artillery, while the 28th Cavalry was to proceed through the foothills to the south and attack from the right flank. The armoured train was to advance along the line in support, while the Turkman cavalry, with the co-operation of that wily bandit Aziz Khan, whose services had been enlisted by Oraz Sirdar, were to block the enemy's line of retreat by cutting the railway north-east of Dushakh.

While this plan was being formulated at the front, the Committee at Ashkhabad was undergoing one of its periodical crises. The shortage of food, brought about by the loss of Merv, was acute, and the railway workers, who were responsible in the first place for the revolt against

Tashkent, were once more showing signs of restiveness. To add to these difficulties, the fall of Baku on September 14th had reduced the Committee, never sure of themselves, to a state of near panic, which manifested itself in repressive legislation and a witch-hunt against those suspected of Bolshevik sympathies. This was conducted with the ruthlessness characteristic of Russian police action, thus lowering the prestige of the Committee in the eyes of the railway workers and others who were revolutionary in their outlook if opposed to the regime in Tashkent. It was widely rumoured that the action taken by Funtikov and his colleagues was being undertaken in response to British orders, an impression that gained acceptance among those who looked upon the British as interlopers, and which Funtikov did little to counteract. As became clear later, the Transcaspian leader took care to cover his actions by spreading the rumour than he acted under pressure from Malleson and his representatives in Ashkhabad.

8

Reactions at Tashkent

ABOUT the same time that the Malleson Mission arrived in Meshed another British Mission to Tashkent was on its way to the Soviet Turkistan capital from Kashgar in the Chinese province of Sinkiang. The British Consul-General in Kashgar, in the person of Sir George Macartney, was admirably placed to observe the confused situation across the border in Turkistan where a Muslim native revolt against the Bolsheviks was gathering force.

Macartney was on the point of retirement, and despite chaotic conditions had hoped to be able to make the return journey to England via Russia instead of travelling by the difficult mountain road through Chitral and India. His successor, Colonel Etherton, had arrived in Kashgar, accompanied by two officers whose mission was to report on the situation in Central Asia and, if possible, to establish contact with the new regime in Tashkent.

As we have seen, the Tashkent Soviet government derived its main support from the Russian railway workers and factory hands in Tashkent and other towns, and from soldiers of the former military garrison. To all of these the native Muslim intelligentzia of the towns and the Kirghiz and Kazakh leaders who were rallying the nomad tribes in their struggle for freedom against Russian oppression were no less obnoxious than officers and officials of the Tsarist government had been. Betrayed by the Russian revolutionary leaders in Turkistan, the native Muslim population, still smarting from the ruthless crushing of a revolt against the military regime of General Kuropatkin in 1916 and more recently from the suppression by the Tashkent Soviet of a Muslim autonomous government at Kokand, had turned against the 'Red' successors of the Tsarist regime, who were, if anything, even more chauvinistic and autocratic than officials of the former Tsarist government had been.

The sending of a British mission to Tashkent, via Kashgar, in

August 1918, without informing its members of developments in Trans-caspia, is indicative of the lack of co-ordination that prevailed at Simla at that time. Difficulties of communication between India and Kashgar may have been partly responsible for the failure to keep the Consul-General at Kashgar fully informed, but it seems hardly likely that no information regarding the Transcaspian revolt against Tash-kent could have reached Kashgar via India by the beginning of August. Colonel F. M. Bailey, a Political Officer of wide experience in Tibet and the frontier regions of India, and Captain L. V. Blacker, a 'Guides' officer, left India for Kashgar via Gilgit in April. The existence of Austro-Hungarian and German prisoners of war in Turkistan, the store of cotton and the threat of an enemy advance along the Central Asian railway were all matters that exercised the minds of the military staff in India and on which information was needed. On the arrival of the party in Kashgar on June 7th, Bailey spent several weeks making a survey of the situation beyond the Turkistan border. At that time Malleson was still in Simla, and there was as yet no sign of any revolt against the Bolsheviks in Transcaspia, although tribal disturbances were already taking place throughout Turkistan.

After consultation with the Consul-General Colonel Bailey decided to make an effort to reach Tashkent and establish direct contact with the authorities there in the hope that some understanding might be reached with them regarding the war prisoners and the disposal of cotton stocks. It was estimated that only by going to Tashkent could a clear picture be obtained of a very confused situation. Sanction having been obtained from Simla, Bailey and Blacker left Kashgar for Tashkent on July 24th, and arrived at the Turkistan capital on August 14th. A few days later they were joined by Sir George Macartney.[1]

Their departure from Kashgar thus took place some ten days after the revolt of the railwaymen in Kizyl Arvat and the change-over in Ashkha-bad, and the beginning of fighting along the railway at Charzhou. A less propitious time to enter into negotiations with Kolesov, the head of the Tashkent Soviet, could hardly have been chosen. News of the arrival of British forces on the Transcaspian frontier had reached Tashkent, so that the Mission, which was without any knowledge of recent events in Transcaspia, was placed in a position of acute em-barrassment, and was unable to make any progress in their talks with Kolesov and his colleagues.

Macartney returned to Kashgar with Blacker, who was ill, but as the situation in Tashkent at that time was extremely tense, and the Turkistan Soviet government in a state of near panic, expecting to be crushed between the advancing Transcaspians and Dutov, Bailey decided to remain behind in hiding, estimating that if the local Soviet collapsed his presence as a British representative might prove useful. Unfortunately, he possessed no sure means of communication with Kashgar, and was entirely dependent on his own ingenuity to escape detection, while keeping himself informed of what was taking place.

Colonel Bailey's subsequent adventures, and his eventual escape from Tashkent, disguised as an Austrian prisoner of war, and his journey across the desert to Sarakhs via Bukhara, are vividly described in his book *Mission to Tashkent*. His presence in Tashkent, in disguise, for more than a year, his meeting while there with some of the leading spirits in the revolt against Bolshevik authority, and his dramatic escape to Meshed through Bukhara, have become something of a legend in Soviet histories of the period.

In Soviet accounts, Colonel Bailey, together with the American Consul Tredwell, are credited with the role of having inspired and directed revolts against the Soviet, of having entered into agreement with 'White Guard' organizations for the 'colonization' of Turkistan by the British government and of having encouraged and supported the Basmachi rebellion.

The ubiquity and influence attributed to Colonel Bailey in the Soviet legend are a tribute to the mystery which surrounded his movements and the ability with which he escaped detection when in hiding at Tashkent.

His presence in Tashkent was quite unknown to the Meshed Mission for some time after the return of the rest of the party to Kashgar. No contact with him was ever established by Meshed, nor did any message from him reach the Mission until he was well on his way to Sarakhs.

Among the Soviet charges made against Colonel Bailey is that he entered into a conspiracy with one Djunkovsky, an ex-official of the Tsarist government, to promote a rebellion against the Soviet government in Turkistan by a 'White' organization known as the Turkistan Military Organization.

Bailey gives no account of ever having met Djunkovsky, who was in

Transcaspia during the summer of 1918. In the early part of July 1918 Djunkovsky arrived in Meshed, and made himself known to the British military attaché, to whom he outlined an elaborate scheme for the co-ordination of anti-Bolshevik activities in Turkistan. As the military attaché was less interested in Russian counter-revolutionary schemes than in securing intelligence concerning the enemy advance through the Caucasus and the situation at Krasnovodsk and along the Central Asian railway, he gave Djunkovsky no encouragement, and on the arrival of the Malleson Mission passed him over to one of the Mission officers. Djunkovsky provided information of value regarding the situation in Turkistan, but his projects aroused no enthusiasm in the mind of the Mission officer who, in any case, was sceptical as to Djunkovsky's ability to perform what he declared his willingness to undertake. As there seemed to be a possibility, however, that Djunkovsky might be of some service to the new regime in Ashkhabad, he was advised to place his services at their disposal.

This was the extent of the connection with Djunkovsky, who left for Ashkhabad a few days later. It seems unlikely that he was able to establish contact with his friends in Tashkent, as the Transcaspian military force was driven back from Chardzhou a few days after his arrival in Ashkhabad, and any link that may have existed through Bukhara would have been slow and uncertain.

Many such projects were submitted to officers of Malmiss from time to time. In most cases the authors of these schemes represented themselves as leaders or important and influential members of organizations aiming at the overthrow of Bolshevism in Central Asia. The provision of funds, arms and ammunition was invariably put forward as a primary requirement. The organizations concerned, whether genuine or projected, having no government to support them, and representing opposition movements with negative programmes, were invariably declared as being willing to dispose of political sovereignty over large tracts of Russian territory, and even urged that the British government should enter into treaty arrangements with them. In no single case were any of these schemes seriously considered, and no arrangement was ever made which involved or inferred support to their promoters. Of these offers, the only one which promised nothing but goodwill and loyalty, and in which no question of funds was raised, was the request made on several occasions by Turkman leaders for British support and even British suzerainty. The only agreements entered into by Malmiss was that reached with the Ashkhabad government for provisional support, and a minor one, by arrangement with the Ashkhabad government, for the provision of a small quantity of small-arms and ammunition to the Emir of Bukhara. No *quid pro quo* was demanded. In this case the arms were delivered, in circumstances which will be described later.

It is part of the Soviet legend regarding events in Russian Central Asia during the revolutionary period that British official support was given to all and sundry among the various counter-revolutionary groups; that 'treaties' involving the disposal of Russian territory or transfer of sovereignty were entered into with certain of them and that British officers were sent as advisors and instructors to the Khanates of Bukhara and Khiva. None was sent to either of these places, and contact made in Ashkhabad and Bairam Ali with representatives of the Bukharan government by members of Malleson's staff was utilized for Intelligence purposes only, or to reassure the Turkman leaders that their wishes were not being completely ignored. No contact was established with Khiva.

The fiction of a treaty having been arrived at between the British Government, or its representatives, and the White counter-revolutionary 'Turkistan Military Organization' providing for a fifty-year British protectorate over Russian Turkistan, derives from articles published in the Soviet newspaper *Pravda* in November 1922 and June 1923, and subsequently repeated, with many embellishments, in other Soviet publications. This story has become part of the stock-in-trade of Soviet historians of the revolutionary period in Turkistan, and like many similar stories of the civil-war period it will doubtless continue to be accepted without question by the Soviet reader until future Soviet historians are able to substitute objective statement for the 'party line' or fanciful assertion.[2]

The Battle of Dushakh

PREPARATIONS for an attack on the enemy position at Dushakh were now well in hand. The supply line from Meshed to Ashkhabad was in operation, but the Malmiss force was still mainly dependent on the Transcaspian Committee for provisions, medical arrangements and transport. Every possible step was being taken to remedy this state of affairs, not only because of the shortage of supplies in Transcaspia but also to assure the Committee that the British were performing their part of the bargain. So far the Transcaspians had fulfilled their part of the bargain, but the behaviour of their troops at the front and the poor staff work displayed, as well as the ineptitude shown in their public administration, did not inspire confidence in their ability to deal adequately with a serious crisis, should one arise.

In their relations with representatives of the Mission the Committee were cordial and co-operative. Many of their difficulties were of their own making, particularly in regard to finance and the organization of supplies. Committee members and officials of proletarian origin and outlook were distrustful towards others with a bourgeois background, and their growing dependence on the support of the latter and, above all, on re-employed ex-officers, irked them. In their social outlook, as well as in their estimation of the world at large, they differed only in degree from their former Bolshevik associates. The Socialist-Revolutionaries were perhaps less obsessed with Marxist ideology; their national patriotism was sincere, if muddled and emotional; and their 'Right wing' favoured continued collaboration with the Allies in prosecuting the war against the Central Powers and, in particular, the Turks.

Among all parties, in fact, in all sections of the population except possibly the Turkman, there was a considerable degree of suspicion of the British which derived from the historical Anglo-Russian rivalry in Persia and in the Central-Asian area generally. This attitude towards the British was more widespread in Russian Turkistan than was anti-Russian sentiment among British military and official circles in India, where it had largely subsided after the signing of the Anglo-Russian Agreement in 1907. Among the Indian population it is doubtful if it ever existed at all, or, at least, not since the time of the Afghan war in 1878, when the 'Russian bear' was a favourite subject for caricaturists and political writers, in India as well as in England. Among Russians, however, suspicion persisted. Isolated from the main current of affairs, and surrounded by a sullen, if not actively hostile, native population, Russian officials and settlers in Turkistan continued to suspect the hand of 'perfidious Albion' in local disturbances and in the tortuous politics of Kabul and Tehran.

In existing circumstances Malleson's relationship with the government and people of Transcaspia was based on the respective needs of both parties. For the British Mission the relationship was provisional and 'for the period of hostilities', and as far as was possible Malleson tried to avoid enmeshment in the internal affairs of the Ashkhabad Committee. For the latter, too, it was equally provisional, but many of them suspected British motives while accepting their bounty, and some, at least, did not hesitate to malign and seek to place responsibility for their own actions and shortcomings on the British when the tide turned against them.

These reservations in mutual relations, however, did not obtrude themselves in the co-operation between the respective military staffs. Former officers of the Russian army now held the key posts on the Transcaspian army staff and in the field, and manned the more efficient units such as the artillery and machine-gun sections. Between them and their British comrades-in-arms relations were good. They did not disguise their admiration for Indian and British troops, and in their reports were generous in their appreciation.

One of the most difficult problems in preparing for the attack was in preserving secrecy. It was reasonable to assume that the Tashkent military staff would not be unaware that preparations were in progress on the Transcaspian side. There were Bolshevik sympathizers in Ashkhabad and Merv, and leakage through agents on the Persian side of the border, as well as from deserters at the front, had to be considered. To counter this, rumours of the impending arrival of large-scale reinforcements, of projected wide encircling movements and of the impending arrival of aircraft and heavy guns were spread about and infiltrated into the Tashkent camp.

To the relief of all concerned, no counter-move was made by the 'Red' Army when the Transcaspian main column moved out across the desert on the night of October 12th. One company of the 1/4 Hampshire Regiment was left in reserve at Kaakha, while the main force of infantry and artillery advanced to a position in a ruined village, Nauroz Chashmeh, several miles north-east of the enemy line at Dushakh. Two squadrons of the 28th Cavalry advanced under cover of the hills south of the railway, while the Turkman cavalry was assigned to make a wide detour to cut the railway in the rear of the enemy's main position.

The main column consisted of two companies of the 19th Punjabis, about 400 Transcaspian infantry and about the same number of Turkman infantry. The British battery of artillery accompanied the main body, being joined later by two Russian guns.

The troops got into position without mishap, but in the early hours of the morning an unfortunate incident aroused the enemy outposts. Two patrols of the 19th Punjabis clashed in the dark, and the firing that ensued gave the alarm to the enemy, thus enabling them to take up defensive positions before the main attack was made. Nevertheless, it was decided to go ahead according to plan, and in the early morning the main Transcaspian force deployed about a mile from the enemy position, the Russians on the right, the Punjabis in the centre and the Turkman infantry on the left.

The ground offered little cover, so that casualties were heavy during the advance against machine-gun fire from trenches and behind irrigation canals on the left of the railway. The Transcaspian Russian and Armenian troops hesitated to advance, taking such cover as they could find, while the Turkman infantry simply disappeared into the desert. With the support of the guns which were shelling the station and Bolshevik troop trains, and accompanied by a number of Russian officers, the Punjabis attacked with the bayonet and in a few minutes drove the enemy out of their line, capturing six guns and sixteen machine-guns. The Bolshevik troops fled to the hills, where they were met by the 28th Cavalry and decimated.

While this operation was in progress, the Bolsheviks succeeded in moving one armoured train eastward, but it was blocked by the Turkman patrol (which incidentally had failed to cut the railway line), and its crew and many fleeing 'Red' soldiers killed. Two other armoured trains moved out of the station westwards, but before any action could be taken to hold them up, a lucky shell hit an ammunition wagon at the station causing an explosion which completely wrecked the station and the rolling stock nearby, killing a large number of enemy troops.

The Transcaspian troops, who had regained their courage by this time, together with a number of Turkman soldiers who reappeared as suddenly as they had departed, arrived on the scene and proceeded to loot what was left of the trains and stores near the station buildings. Taking advantage of the confusion, the Bolsheviks rallied, additional troops having been brought up from Tedzhen, the two armoured trains backing towards the station. Only the Punjabis, who had suffered heavy casualties, remained in action, and once more they attacked with the bayonet. The 28th Cavalry now appeared on the scene. The enemy, badly shaken by the Punjabis and the 28th Cavalry attack, fell back, leaving a quantity of war material and all stores that had not been destroyed in the explosion.

Although the cavalry were prepared to follow up the retreat, it was decided in view of the demoralized and uncontrollable state of the Transcaspian troops to withdraw to Kaakha. All wounded were evacuated, and the whole force retreated to its previous position that night. Any counter-attack from the direction of Dushakh seemed unlikely, but precautions had been taken to remove sections of the rails in case an enemy armoured train should attempt it.

British and Indian casualties were very heavy in this action. The 19th Punjabis lost all their British officers, killed or wounded, and forty-seven killed and 139 wounded among other ranks. The 28th Cavalry lost six killed and eleven wounded. Transcaspian losses were seven killed and thirty wounded. Enemy losses were at least 1,000 killed and wounded.

Once again the lack of discipline and fighting quality on the part of the Transcaspians, the unreliability of the Turkman troops and their propensity for looting, prevented a decisive battle being fought. This was readily admitted in the official report published in the Ashkhabad Press several days later, in which full credit was given to the Indian and British troops, and the pusillanimity of their own soldiers (with some exceptions) was deplored. Amends for this state of affairs were promised, but, as will appear later, little was done to improve the quality of their own men.

It was expected that the Bolsheviks would evacuate the Dushakh position which had now become untenable for their trains. On the night of October 17th they evacuated Dushakh and withdrew to Tedzhen. Evidently fearing a flanking attack from the 28th Cavalry, they withdrew farther eastward to Merv on the 23rd and began to remove the rest of the war material remaining at Kushk. A few days later, threatened by a flanking movement which was little more than a patrol action, they fled precipitately from Merv towards Chardzhou. The Transcaspian force advanced to Merv and preparations were made to follow up the enemy retreat.

At this moment instructions were received by General Malleson from the Government of India forbidding British troops to advance beyond the Merv oasis. The reasons for this order were not vouchsafed, but were undoubtedly connected with the threatening situation in Afghanistan, disinclination or inability to provide reinforcements and perhaps questions of higher policy.

In response to General Malleson's request, however, he was promised a general officer as commander of the British force, and three staff officers, to be under General Malleson's command, but to set up their headquarters at Ashkhabad or at the front as was thought fit.

The remaining company of Punjabis and one squadron of cavalry were sent to the front, their duties on the northern section of the Cordon being taken over by two companies of the 2/98th Punjabis sent from Seistan. Additional supply and transport officers and several officer replacements for the casualties sustained at Dushakh were also sent from Quetta.

The defeat inflicted on the Bolsheviks at Dushakh was even more severe than was estimated at the time. Thoroughly demoralized, they fled towards Chardzhou, and were evidently prepared to abandon that position. Had it been possible to follow up their retreat in force, there is little doubt that the bridge and town at Chardzhou could have captured, with incalculable effects on the campaign. From reports received a little later from Tashkent, the government there was in a state of alarm and began to clamour for assistance from Moscow. All foreigners of Allied nationality were arrested, and the usual round-up of suspects was carried out. The reputation of the Indian troops infected the whole 'Red' Army, and exaggerated reports of their numbers, their allegedly superior equipment and their ferocity were made public to justify the set-back the 'Red' Army had suffered.

Despite the prohibition against British troops participating in any advance beyond the Merv area, Oraz Sirdar rather rashly decided to follow up the 'Red' retreat, and armoured trains with infantry and artillery crept cautiously up the line towards Chardzhou. The Bolsheviks had established an advanced line at their old position at Uch Aji, but this did not appear to be strongly held.

On November 14th the premature burst of a shell set off an explosion in an ammunition wagon, causing panic among the train-crew which quickly spread to the troops. Enemy shelling, probably stimulated by the explosion and the smoke and noise, added to the confusion and the whole force turned tail and retreated to Annenkovo, 100 miles to the rear. At this point there was shelter for the armoured train, and sand-dunes for cover, but no natural advantages for a strong defensive position. After a pause to recover from their astonishment, the Bolsheviks advanced their own armoured trains to Ravnina, a few miles east of Annenkovo, but made no attempt to follow up their gain. Evidently fearing a flank attack, and with no stomach to face Indian bayonets and machine-gun fire again, they confined themselves to occasional artillery fire for some weeks to come.

By this time winter had set in, and troops on both sides, at the front-line positions, took to the shelter of their trains. Snow and freezing winds brought operations to a standstill. Deprived of British help for a further advance, and deterred by the low morale of his own troops, Oraz Sirdar decided to sit it out in the hope that the British order might be rescinded and that help would be forthcoming from beyond the Caspian where Denikin's troops were advancing towards the sea.

Soviet historians fumble a little in apportioning the blame for the near débâcle at Dushakh. Superior British and Transcaspian numbers; heavier artillery; Aziz Khan's threat to their rear; and faulty command and planning—all these are alleged. Some accounts even refer to the presence of a mythical Scottish battalion. One Soviet writer alleges that

4,000 British troops were engaged in Transcaspia. The only British troops (excluding the gallant Indians) in the fight were a few artillerymen and the British officers of the 19th Punjabis and 28th Cavalry and several staff officers. The total strength of the British-Indian force at the front was at that time about 500 officers and men. At no time was the British-Indian force in Transcaspia greater in numbers than 1,000 officers and men.

But for the poor quality of the Ashkhabad forces and the behaviour of the Turkman troops, the 'Red' defeat at Dushakh might have proved decisive; as it happened, it gave Merv and the oasis area back to the Transcaspian government and staved off the economic crisis that was beginning to strangle their efforts to stabilize their position.[1]

The improvised nature of the chain of command and liaison between the British and Transcaspian forces no longer met the needs of the situation. Malleson's troops, although under Oraz Sirdar for operational purposes, had no unified command of their own. Malleson therefore requested his chiefs in Delhi to hasten the appointment of a senior officer to command the two regiments and details at the front. Brigadier-General G. Beatty, who had led Indian troops in France and Egypt and who was now in Lucknow, was immediately appointed to the post and was expected to arrive in Meshed towards the end of November.

In preparation for the changes in command, and for the reorganization of the whole defensive situation in the light of the collapse of the Turkish threat to Persia and Transcaspia, a staff conference of the British detachments and the East Persian Cordon was called to take place in Meshed at the end of November.

Meshed

MESHED in 1918 was a city of about 100,000 people, nearly a quarter of which were Turkmans, Afghans and tribesmen of various kinds. As the capital of the province of Khorasan, it had a Governor, a Prince of the Royal Family and a garrison of several thousand Persian troops, some of whom belonged to the so-called Persian Cossack Brigade, commanded by Russian officers. Unlike other east Persian towns, Meshed contained a small European community, mainly Russian. The Governor lived in a state of provincial magnificence, and was provided with a bodyguard whose uniforms and accoutrements, more for show than for use, were a living example of Thorstein Veblen's theory of 'Conspicuous waste'. The army, apart from its officers, who were attired in a showy uniform of Austrian type, lacked provision; the ragged infantry, ill-fed and seldom paid, eked out their dreary existence in the dusty barracks facing the Maidan or public square, appearing in small parties, accompanied by a brass band (which had only one tune), on festive occasions or at public executions. It seemed doubtful that their warlike capacities would exceed those of the armies described in Morier's *Hadji Baba* or of Falstaff's ragged crew on the road to Shrewsbury.

The official quarter of Meshed had a vaguely European air; a few solid buildings; a spacious Maidan, a park and several handsome Consulate houses contrasted with the narrow lanes and walled-in houses of the rest of the city. Russian influence was in evidence, especially in the bazaar, which still contained Russian goods, many booths and shops having Russian as well as Persian signs.

A small European community, stimulated by the presence of the British Mission and lulled into a sense of comparative security, had embarked on the round of dinners, receptions and parties with which exiled Europeans in an Eastern country endeavour to compensate for their sense of isolation. Apart from the British Consular and military staffs, the former Russian Consul-General, M. Nikolsky, with his military attaché Colonel Baratov, General Guschin, a retired Russian officer, who had formerly commanded a unit of the Persian Cossack Brigade, a Russian doctor, a bank manager and several other Russian officers, formed a small but agreeable group of their own. Several Belgian officials of the Persian Customs Department (at that time most Persian fiscal, Customs and police organizations were directed by foreigners) and the Swedish commandant of the Persian Gendarmerie, Captain Janson, constituted another 'official' group.

As there was little industry in the town except carpet-making, and that on a small scale, the principal source of income seemed to be pilgrims to the Bast, or Holy Shrine, of which more than 100,000 were reputed to visit the city every year, coming from as far afield as India, Mesopotamia and the Persian-speaking parts of Afghanistan and Turkistan. Dating back to the tenth century, when the city was known as Sanabad, the original building surrounded the tomb of the great Caliph of Bagdad, Haroun al-Rashid, of Arabian Nights fame, who died there. A years or so after Haroun al-Rashid's death, Prince Ali Resa, twelfth in descent from the Prophet, died mysteriously in Sanabad and was buried close to the tomb of the Caliph. The tomb of Ali became the shrine of Ali, now the sacred Imam Reza of the Shia Muslims. Sanabad became Meshed, a 'place of martyrdom', and one of the most revered places in Persia. By the fourteenth century Meshed had become a place of importance, the shrine having become known throughout the Shia world as the richest and most magnificent of all Persian places of pilgrimage.

The temper of the people of Meshed had become more fanatical than is normal with Persians, probably due to the influx of pilgrims and the wild ceremonies depicting the murder of the holy figures of Shia Islam, Hussein and Hassan, which were a feature of the religious life of the city.

In the year 1911 Russian troops had invaded the holy precincts, and the golden dome of the Bast was damaged by shell fire, an act of sacrilege which still burnt in the hearts of the people of Khorasan.

As a Shia shrine, the Bast possessed no special significance for the Sunni Muslim population, whose rejection of the Shia claims on behalf of the murdered Imams is as absolute as that of the rejection by the early Western church of the heresies of Alexandria and Asia Minor.

At the time of the events described in these pages there was much poverty and distress in the city, and when epidemic or famine struck the well-to-do betook themselves to more favoured regions, leaving their dependents and others to fend for themselves. Suffering from a long period of misgovernment and subjected to outside pressures and intervention by foreign Powers, Persia had lapsed into a state of apathy and official neglect, from which the country and its long-suffering people were not to emerge until an energetic leader arose to sweep away much dead wood and infuse energy and self-respect into the nation.

During the summer of 1918 the Meshed bazaar was full of rumours of Turkish victories, of alleged British atrocities in Mesopotamia and of British hostility towards Islam. These stemmed from Turkish propaganda conducted through the 'Caucasian Committee' which at that time was active in the town. The Mission immediately took counter-action by the production of a daily news-sheet, and by bringing representative Muslims from Arabia, Mesopotamia and India to testify to the true state of affairs. The success of Turkish propaganda, and, at a later date, of Bolshevik propaganda, in some parts at least of the Muslim world, seemed to be less due to the efficiency of its promoters than to the absence of any effective British counter-propaganda organization. Defamation of the British, and misrepresentation of Allied aims and policies, past and present, had a clear field until missions such as Malmiss took counter-steps, largely on their own initiative. Such action was local in its effect, but served its purpose at the time.[1]

News reaching the bazaars of east Persia and Afghanistan was tainted at the source, and distorted in the telling. Persian newspapers printed the bulletins of both sides, but the emphasis was on enemy successes and stories of alleged instances of British hostility towards Islam.

The Mission news-sheet was supplemented by distribution of news-papers and illustrated magazines, some with Persian captions, containing news of events abroad and short articles by Arab, Egyptian and Syrian writers. The news bulletin, which started with a single sheet, was now increased to four or five sheets, and contained material which was daily gathered from wireless news-services throughout the world. If not all Malmiss bulletins were believed, effective competition with the rather clumsy productions of the Caucasian Committee, and the rumours spread by enemy agents, soon began to show results. These efforts on the part of the Mission were conducted at first with complete disregard for the susceptibilities of the Persians, but as time went on consideration was also given to their needs and difficulties.

Apart from day-to-day information derived from field-wireless intercepts and sources in Transcaspia, the Mission's own intelligence network, now being extended to outposts in Sarakhs, Kuchan, Shahrud, Asterabad and Kahriz (on the road to Herat), and penetrating behind the Bolshevik lines to Chardzhou, Samarkand and Tashkent, began to bring in a steady flow of news.

The Persian government, officially neutral, but embarrassed by the presence on Persian soil of troops of both sides, took no steps to check or counter the propaganda activities of either party. Public sympathies varied with the class, status, occupation and location of its members. The prestige of the combatants fluctuated with their fortunes, but Turkish propaganda, emanating from an Islamic country, albeit Sunni, possessed an advantage over that of the Allies. A considerable proportion of the population of Persia is of non-Persian race, and includes many Afghans, Turkmans, Caucasian Tartars and nomad tribesmen who were more susceptible than the Shia Persians to propaganda and to ideas disseminated by enemy propagandists.

This situation was now suddenly changed by news of the Turkish collapse, followed a few days later by the capitulation of Austria and Germany. This came as something of an anticlimax to the Mission in Meshed. The chief reason for the presence of a British Mission in north-east Persia, namely the threat of an enemy advance across the Caspian towards India, disappeared with the collapse of Turkey on October 30th. British involvement in the affairs of Transcaspia, derived from this threat, had somewhat changed its character as a result of the hostile relations that had developed between the Soviet government and Russia's former allies. The reasons for this hostility and in particular for the attitude of the Allied governments towards the Bolshevik regime, are many and varied, and likely to remain subjects for dispute for many years to come. The decisions reached at Versailles early in 1919 to support anti-Bolshevik armies were, however, based on quite different considerations from those which actuated the Government of India and the Army Command at Bagdad to send military missions to north Persia in 1918. In the latter case the moves were tactical, their original purpose being fulfilled with the collapse of the the enemy. Their involvement in Russian revolutionary affairs was accidental and even reluctant, although this will be disputed by Russian historians. But having become involved, the problem of disengagement was not an easy one, and was to become even more complicated as wider political issues came up for discussion at the Peace Conference tables.

Malleson's planning had envisaged the maintenance of two fronts for some time to come; a holding operation against the Tashkent Bolsheviks to enable him to keep control of the Central Asian railway and the port of Krasnovodsk, and co-operation with other British forces in the Caspian area to block Turkish passage across the Caspian into Central Asia and into north Persia.

Suddenly, with little warning, all this planning lost its significance, and the stimulus of planned operations was displaced by the uncertainties of future policy. The ending of the war for those in England, and for armies on the main fronts, was a release of tension and the removal of the fears and anxieties induced by the prospect of another winter of warfare. But for those who were on remote outpost duty in completely alien surroundings, and cut off from the main course of events, the real significance of the ending of the war was not at first realized. It appeared to make little local impact; people were either indifferent or had little understanding of an event so remote from themselves. The pro-Turk element had been caught off guard, and made an effort to misrepresent the news as false.

Within a few days of the Turkish capitulation, the advance party of a British occupation force from Enzeli under the command of General Thompson arrived at Baku where a new provisional Azerbaijan government had assumed power.

The detachment at Krasnovodsk was also strengthened by a naval unit, and several steamers were armed as a precaution against a revival of hostilities in the Caspian.[2]

The reoccupation of Baku by British troops in November was

strongly protested against by Moscow, the charge being made that their presence there was actuated by a desire to secure control of the oil industry and extend British influence in Transcaucasia.

General Thompson's orders were to maintain law and order, ensure the evacuation of the surrendered Turkish army and in due course to hand over the civil administration to the legally elected local authority.

A provincial government, anti-Bolshevik in character and aiming at Azerbaijan independence, took control of public affairs, remaining in power until replaced by a more stable regime, which continued to function during the period of British occupation, after which it was eventually replaced by a Bolshevik administration when Soviet Russian forces from Astrakhan took possession of the city.[3]

The Move to Ashkhabad

WITH the relatively stabilized position of the Merv front, the Turko-German threat to Transcaspia removed and contact re-established with Baku, Malleson decided to move his headquarters temporarily to Ashkhabad. Supply arrangements were now beginning to function smoothly. The road to Ashkhabad was now in fair working order and guarded by levies under the command of Captain Geidt, an Indian army officer with a genius for handling raw tribesmen and turning them into soldiers. Convoys of *fourgons* and cars made the journey several times a week, and with the establishment of transport depots at Kuchan and Bajgiran (the latter under joint management with the Russians) there were few delays from breakdowns of vehicles.

In view of the uncertain position regarding the further role of British troops in Transcaspia, it was essential that Malleson should meet members of the Committee and Army Command, and inspect the British-Indian force at the front.

After the experience of Kaakha and Dushakh the question of the chain of command had to be examined on the spot. With the bulk of the forces at Malleson's disposal now in Transcaspia or on the way there, a local field commander was necessary, but before General Beatty took up his post the working of the new arrangement would have to be discussed with Oraz Sirdar and the two British regimental commanders, Colonel Knollys and Colonel Hawley. The arrival of British artillery and infantry units from Dunsterforce, and their posting to Krasnovodsk, Ashkhabad and Merv, also necessitated talks to resolve questions of command and supply.

The restriction imposed by Simla on the movement of British troops east of the Merv oasis area would, it was realized, inevitably lead to difficulties with the Committee. This order could not fail to be interpreted by them as a clear indication that the British were solely concerned with their own political and strategic interests and were about to abandon their Transcaspian allies, notwithstanding the fact that the British were in conflict with Bolshevik forces elsewhere.

With British troops back in Baku, and growing opposition to the Bolshevik regime in Russia, it would be urged that a local withdrawal would not make sense, particularly at a time when the various anti-Bolshevik armies were making progress, Kolchak in Siberia, and the volunteer army in south Russia and the north Caucasus.

At that time the question of Allied intervention, apart from the precautionary occupation of Murmansk and tactical military moves undertaken in the war against the Central Powers and Turkey, had not yet been determined as a matter of agreed policy, but hopes were entertained in many quarters that the Bolshevik regime would shortly collapse, or that with the end of the European war some kind of settlement would be reached that would safeguard the interests of all parties.

The Socialist-Revolutionary and Menshevik leaders shared this illusion, and continued to place their hopes on the calling of an All-Russian Constituent Assembly, which they vainly supposed would sort out all their political differences and produce a democratic constitution acceptable to the whole Russian nation.

That this would be hindered, on the one hand by Bolshevik determination to keep power in their own hands, and on the other by Russian incapacity for compromise, was yet to be seen. But the inability of members of the various opposition groups to see any point of view but their own, their contentiousness and tendency to faction, even when faced with the ruthlessness and single-mindedness of the Bolshevik creed, hardly disposed Allied governments to view them with any degree of confidence. If Russia were not to be ruled by a Bolshevik dictatorship it seemed certain that it would be faced with a second 'Time of Troubles', as none of the numerous parties in opposition to Communist rule seemed able to produce a concrete programme of action, or the will to exercise authority. The lack of experience of practical politics and administration, the result of the Tsarist centralization of government and exclusion of 'intellectuals' and members of the educated middle class in general from local government and public affairs, rendered the liberal and moderate socialist leaders incapable of undertaking the practical tasks of government and administration.

Their energies were wasted in factional disputes and in theoretical discussion.

This state of affairs prevailed in Transcaspia and Baku as elsewhere in the territory of the former Tsarist Empire where civil-war conditions existed. Party leaders argued interminably and quarrelled over obscure points of socialist theory, while the Bolsheviks, as yet seriously unhampered by doctrinal dissension, adopted, with Machiavellian subtlety, the principles of power politics, using force whenever argument failed to achieve its object.

In Transcaspia the Committee and its adherents, conscious of their weakness, sought to thrust on to the British full responsibility for the defence of the region against Tashkent, as well as against potential enemies from Astrakhan and Baku. Although willing to provide the material support promised to Ashkhabad, General Malleson was equally determined to avoid being more deeply embroiled in Transcaspian domestic affairs than he could help. The instructions sent to Malleson from India at the end of November, placing a limit on the advance of British troops, clearly indicated that the Government of India had no intention of becoming more deeply involved in the morass of Turkistan.[1] In India the implications of the revolt of the native Muslim population against the Bolshevik regime in Tashkent were not yet fully appreciated. It was generally regarded as stemming from pan-Islamic agitation, and thus of interest mainly in relation to developments in Afghanistan and the North-West Frontier.

While reassuring the Committee that no immediate withdrawal was contemplated, Malleson was compelled to resist firmly but tactfully all attempts by the Transcaspians to make Malmiss responsible for domestic problems, or for internal security measures.

A few days before the arrival in Ashkhabad of the Mission from Meshed a plot to overthrow the government had been frustrated by swift action on the part of Drushkin, the chief of police. A demand for an increase of pay by the railwaymen had been followed by a threat to strike, and meetings had taken place in Ashkhabad and other centres at which anti-government speeches had been made. A number of people had been arrested and others placed under surveillance, but the threat to bring the railway to a standstill remained unless funds could be found to satisfy the demands of the railwaymen and minor officials.

In response to an appeal to Malleson, a squadron of the 28th Cavalry was sent to Ashkhabad, and General Thompson was requested to authorize the transfer of a platoon of the Royal Warwickshire Regiment from Krasnovodsk to Ashkhabad. The Warwicks were transferred immediately and were installed in the main barracks and armoury to forestall any attempt on the part of insurgents to secure arms.

While the situation at the front was temporarily stabilized, the position of the Committee had deteriorated. It was now confronted by a number of problems with which it was unable to cope unaided. The most urgent of these was the financial situation. The Treasury was depleted; currency was in a state of confusion and inflation was rife. The demand for higher pay on the part of officials and workers, including the all-important railwaymen, could no longer be ignored. Efforts to raise revenue through increased taxation had only partially succeeded and had given rise to public discontent which was being exploited by opposition elements among the workers.

Reoccupation of the Merv area had eased the supply situation, but the cost of commodities had risen by leaps and bounds. Much damage had been inflicted on the inhabitants of the oasis, who were showing reluctance to dispose of their produce for depreciated currency. The bitterness against the Russians, caused by the seizure of Turkman supplies by the Bolsheviks when in occupation of Merv and the surrounding district, precluded steps being taken to requisition surplus stocks or to enforce sales.

Another problem arose from the unsatisfactory state of relations with the Turkman population. While the latter were fiercely anti-Bolshevik, their relations with the Committee had not been clearly defined, in spite of the role played by Oraz Sirdar as commander of the Transcaspian forces. Nationalist sentiment was strong among the Turkman tribesmen; several of their leaders had not disguised their pro-Turk leanings, although this had not interfered with their friendly personal relations with British officers. While the Committee needed Turkman help, its Russian members were hesitant to accord them more representation and voice in public affairs than they then enjoyed.

The question of recruitment for the army was another problem that exercised the Committee, or perhaps it would be more correct to say the Army Command. Avoidance of military service was general, particularly among workmen, both Russian and Armenian, and it was evident that the Committee hoped to overcome the deficiency in this respect by persuading General Malleson to make more troops available.

Many difficulties experienced by the government were due to lack of experience in administration, and to the proliferation of committees which constantly interfered in the carrying out of official and army orders. The government, in accordance with Russian tradition, adopted repressive police action to deal with public discontent, thus providing ammunition for the agitation, largely organized by underground Bolshevik agents, directed against its authority. The chief of police, Drushkin, had tightened up security arrangements which involved a number of arrests, actions which did little to enhance the popularity of the Committee or promote confidence in its ability to alleviate public discontent.

One of the causes of financial stringency was the diversity of currency. Three types of rouble notes were in circulation: the old Tsarist currency, commonly known as 'Nikolaisky'; the Kerensky government issue, taking its name from that short-lived government; and an issue by the Tashkent Soviet government. Persian notes were also in circulation, but these, as well as silver coinage of various currencies, in accordance with Gresham's Law were hoarded, or used only in private transactions.

A 70,000,000 rouble windfall, found in the Treasury by the Committee on taking over from the previous Soviet regime, was now practically exhausted, while the value of the notes had dropped to a fraction of their original value. Curiously enough, 'Nikolaisky' notes, particularly those of high denominations, still had high exchange value. This fluctuated with the success or failure of 'White' army operations elsewhere in Russia. Many millions of roubles in these handsomely printed notes were hoarded by members of the 'bourgeois' class, or traders, in the hope that they would some day regain their full value.

The question of financial assistance by Malmiss had been under examination in Meshed for some weeks past, and had been the subject of much correspondence between the Mission and General Malleson's chiefs at Simla. No definite scheme had as yet been evolved, the main difficulty being that of exchange. The British were now providing their own supplies to their troops in the field, apart from some foodstuffs which were being paid for by roubles purchased for rupee drafts. This was a provisional arrangement which needed to be placed on a firm and agreed basis.

Any issue of notes by the Transcaspian government would need to be backed by bullion, or by some form of guarantee, unless a complete change in the internal political and military situation took place that would enhance the authority and strengthen the stability of the government. It was evident that the problem of exchange would have to be overcome, or some method evolved whereby the credit of the Committee could be stabilized with the least possible delay so that the questions of higher pay and prices could be handled without further loss of prestige.

On questions of administration and police action against subversive elements, it was obviously undesirable that the British Mission should appear to be giving orders to the Committee, or interfering in its domestic affairs. On the other hand, security on the home front was of equal importance with security at the front, so that steps taken by the Committee to check subversion and counteract Bolshevik propaganda was in the interests of both parties. Drushkin, although not a popular official—partly, no doubt, due to his Jewish origin, regarding which there was much prejudice among the Russians of all classes—was energetic and courageous, and less concerned with doctrinaire matters than was the case with most of the Ministers and some of his colleagues. It therefore seemed desirable to discourage any attempt to dislodge him, the obvious aim of the malcontents as well as those who disliked him on personal grounds.

The Committee's failure to secure the service of more volunteers was partly due to its loss of prestige and the deteriorating economic situation. Conscription, although nominally in force, could not be enforced, at any rate against the Russian workers who, even if they had opposed the decrees and methods of Tashkent, had no wish to fight. The old resentment against authority; suspicion of the allegedly reactionary outlook of the officer class; the effects of pacifist and anti-imperialist propaganda; and now suspicion of the aims and motives of the British, fostered by Bolshevik propaganda in their midst, were all elements in the reluctance shown by many Russians, whether Menshevik or Socialist-Revolutionary, to take up arms against the Soviet. The majority of Russians (apart from many officers and officials of the old regime and members of the former upper class) seemed to be opposed to any reversion to the Tsarist regime, and were thus torn between a desire for the re-establishment of law and order and suspicion of any attempt to re-establish by force these essentials to normal living, especially where outside help (or, as many of them regarded it, foreign interference) was involved.

In this particular case the Transcaspian revolt against Bolshevik Tashkent was of their own making. The assistance they sought had been granted, it seemed to General Malleson, on reasonable terms. He had undertaken to assist them militarily and financially but not to relieve them of all responsibility for the defence of their own regime. Failure to reassure the Turkman people was one source of weakness; another was the suspicion shown towards ex-officers and soldiers of the old regime who were fighting at the front; while the size of military establishments in the rear as compared with the strength maintained at the front suggested inability of the government to enforce its orders.

On the Turkman issue it seemed desirable that some assurance should be given to the tribesmen and their leaders that they were not merely fighting for one set of Russians against another set of Russians. The Turkmans, like the Kazakhs, Kirghiz and other Turkistan peoples, wanted some degree of autonomy, and the right, promised them by the Soviet government in the famous declaration of November 15th, 1917, to manage their own affairs. Never reconciled to Russian rule, which they had strenuously resisted during General Skobelev's campaign in the seventies and eighties of the past century (Oraz Sirdar was the son of the defender of the Turkman fortress at Geok-Tepe), they had placed their hopes on the Turks, but now, with the collapse of the Turkish army, they were tentatively putting out feelers to the British.[2]

If full Turkman support to the Ashkhabad government were to be secured, it was essential, as a first step, to grant them more representation in their government, whatever risks were involved, and give them an opportunity to create their own local authorities. Some form of economic assistance was also necessary in view of the depredations of the Bolsheviks and the break-up of their traditional institutions.

Obviously, this was not going to be easy, and British suggestions would inevitably be regarded with suspicion. No encouragement had been given by the British Mission to the Turkman leaders that British help would be forthcoming, other than supporting their claim for wider representation in local government. The main difficulty, apart from Russian suspicion of native aims, lay in the fact that few Turkman tribesmen were educated; they had a nomadic and, in the case of the Tekke tribe, a village mentality. Freedom was in their blood, but it seemed unlikely that they would be capable, in a short time, to work out and sustain their own organization of government. However, the problem was there to be faced, and the attempt would have to be made to encourage the Committee to consider it, as a factor in the recruitment situation and in relation to wider questions of security. Turkman demands were already being made and would come up for discussion; the best that could be done was to put forward suggestions; how they should be implemented was a matter for the government to decide, if indeed the suggestions were not rejected forthwith.

The Committee's desire to have more British troops made available was, of course, linked with their own recruitment problem. Apart from replacement of officer casualties, and the transfer of the rest of the Punjabis and 28th Cavalry to Transcaspia, there seemed now to be very little likelihood of any additional British or Indian troops being made available from Malleson's own limited resources. A few more infantry and artillery and some specialist troops might be provided from Enzeli by General Thompson, but his relatively small force was already fully occupied with maintaining order in Baku and with the difficult task of dislodging the scattered groups of Nuri Pasha's Turkish army from the Caucasus.[3]

The Turkish commander, evidently convinced that the confused situation in the Caucasus still provided opportunities for playing the pan-Turanian game, had announced that his army, which had a considerable number of Azerbaijani volunteers in its ranks, was now in the service of the Azerbaijan government.

The arrest of Nuri Pasha and members of his staff soon put an end to this final effort to exploit local religious and political tension, but some months were to elapse before all Turkish troops were rounded up and disarmed, and placed under guard pending the completion of arrangements for their evacuation from Transcaucasia.

The Executive Committee

THE Transcaspian government consisted of a Board of Directors, five in number. The Board, commonly referred to as the 'Executive Committee', consisted of Funtikov (Chairman of the Committee), Zimen (Foreign Affairs), Kurilov (Labour and Transport) and Dmitrievsky (Finance). The fifth member, General Kruten, was responsible in an advisory capacity for the army, while a Turkman, Hadji Murat, in an *ex-officio* capacity, represented Turkman affairs. Dokhov, who had been closely associated with Funtikov at the time the government was formed, was its liaison officer and representative in Meshed.

None of these men possessed any outstanding qualities of leadership. Funtikov was an aggressive man of the 'Labour leader' type of the old school, without education, and addicted to intrigue. As he had shown in the case of the Twenty-six Commissars, he could be ruthless and vindictive, more through fear than because of strong conviction of the rightness of the course he was pursuing. A heavy drinker, he was alternately jovial and moody, and in the latter state inclined to be suspicious. His authority stemmed from the role he had played in the revolt against Tashkent, and was sustained by an attitude of 'toughness' rather than by a display of moral leadership.

Lev Alexandrovich Zimen, in appearance and manner, suggested a character out of a Chekhov play. Tall and spare, with a short beard and untidy hair, he wore a high collar, a frock-coat of clerical cut and pince-nez, through which he regarded the world with the eyes of a scholar. A schoolmaster, and a well-known Orientalist, he was an authority on Turkistan languages and culture, and had held important academic posts in Tashkent and Merv. By conviction he was a right-wing Socialist-Revolutionary, but like many Russian 'liberals' his ideas ranged far beyond the political programme of his party and would probably have been regarded as unorthodox. A kindly well-meaning

G

man, he was out of his element in the company of tough characters like Funtikov and Kurilov. Zimen was the best-educated man in the Committee, and any authority he possessed stemmed from that fact. He was outwardly friendly towards his British 'allies' and personally open and sincere in his relations with members of the Malmiss Mission, but, *au fond*, he had all the characteristic Russian suspicion of British motives. He had fixed ideas about the iniquity of the British regime in India, which he regarded as 'imperialistic'; but at the same time he somewhat illogically regarded Russian control over the Muslim population of Turkistan as paternalistic and historically justified, although he would agree that the paternalism of General Kuropatkin, the last governor of Turkistan, left something to be desired. At a later date, when arrested in Baku by the Bolsheviks, he tried to place on British shoulders all responsibility for the actions of the Committee, his 'testimony' at his trial forming to this day part of the official Soviet charge of British 'colonialist' ambition in Turkistan.

Kurilov, a colourless man, was similar in type to Dokhov, but with the ruthlessness of Funtikov. Closely linked with the latter, he took an active part in the intrigues which ultimately led to the breakdown of the Committee and its replacement by a Committee of Public Safety.

General Kruten, who had seen service in the Caucasus and Persia, was an attractive old gentleman of liberal views and an almost complete disregard for doctrinaire politics. What he lacked in energy and administrative ability he compensated for in honesty of purpose and personal integrity, both somewhat rare qualities in a revolutionary atmosphere of intrigue and suspicion.

Hadji Murat, one of the few well-educated Turkman leaders, like his colleague Obez Baev, had the reputation of being a strong Turkophile, and there is little doubt that he, like many Turkman leaders, had placed his hopes on Turkish plans to displace the Russians as the rulers of Central Asia. Both he and Obez Baev had been in Tsarist service, but they had little love for the Russians. In his relations with the British Mission he was friendly and courteous, and after the Turkish collapse he was among the Turkman leaders who sought British protection for his people.

The most outstanding personality in Ashkhabad was Simion Lvovich Drushkin, Director of Public Security. A lawyer of Jewish origin, he had escaped from Tashkent at the time of the purge of non-Bolsheviks from the Soviet administration earlier in the year. Drushkin was not unlike Kerensky in appearance: clean-shaven, with a keen, thin face and penetrating eyes. An efficient if ruthless policeman, he was not unnaturally far from popular, and was eyed with suspicion by some members of the Committee, as well as by the leading figures in the various committees that plagued the administration. As will appear later, Drushkin was to play an important role in the political crisis which developed at the end of December.

Another personality who played an effective part behind the scenes was Count Dorrer, a senior official in Zimen's department. Dorrer had been associated with the provisional government regime in Tashkent, and had escaped from that city during the disorders which followed the seizure of power by the Bolsheviks early in the year. A self-effacing man of charming manners, with an attractive wife, he seemed out of place in the company of men of the type of Funtikov and Kurilov, and as a member of the 'bourgeois' class he was suspect in the eyes of the class-conscious Mensheviks and other proletarians who sought to overturn the government in power.

In the wider political sphere it was still too early to form any estimate of the effect of the enemy capitulation in the West. That it would sooner or later alter the *raison d'être* for the presence of British troops in Transcaspia seemed evident, although it was unlikely (or so it was considered at the time) that British commitments to the Transcaspians would be abandoned lightly. The presence of British troops in the country would inevitably come under review in India and in London. Meanwhile there were immediate and practical issues to be solved.[1]

In these circumstances Malleson decided that talks with the Committee should continue on a formal basis, but that for the time being they would be confined to the urgent questions of finance and supply. Preparatory talks on these matters had already taken place between Captain Teague-Jones and Zimen, and the Committee had been requested to produce memoranda setting forth their requirements. Zimen had been pressing for an early decision on the subject of a subsidy by the British as had been promised at the time the agreement was signed in August. During this time various schemes had been under consideration in Meshed, and had been the subject of consultation with the Government of India at Simla. Although Malleson's financial powers were 'unlimited' according to his orders, he was in fact still severely hampered by an acute shortage of cash, and had not found the higher powers in India particularly helpful in devising a workable plan to provide funds for Ashkhabad.

A prerequisite to any effective financial scheme was assurance that the Committee should put its own financial house in order, in so far as it was able to do so. The appointment of a banker, Dmitrievsky, as Director of Finances gave some hope that steps in that direction would be taken, and that there would be effective control over the working of whatever plan would eventually be evolved.

The situation had now become acute, and the Committee was urging that some provisional arrangement be arrived at to tide over the immediate crisis. Owing to exchange and other banking difficulties, a simple bank credit would not meet the case. Malleson and his advisers held strongly to the opinion that whatever method was adopted it should be one that would enable the Transcaspian government to build up its own credit and give it a more or less stable currency. To provide a cash subsidy on any other basis would simply make the British government responsible for the finances of the government and its budget, and compel the Mission to assume responsibility for its internal affairs.

The scheme now under consideration provided for the issue by the Mission of promissory notes for a specified period payable on maturity in roubles. These notes, issued with the authority of the British government, their repayment guaranteed by the British Mission and the Transcaspian government, would circulate as currency during their period of validity, during which time the Transcaspian government would issue its own currency to an agreed amount. At the same time it was proposed that the British Mission would provide a silver bullion reserve to sustain the Transcaspian currency, which, however, would be based on the value of state property and enterprises. At maturity the Transcaspian government would make available roubles of its own currency for repayment of the promissory notes.

In this manner, it was considered, the business community, wage and salary earners, and the public as a whole, would have an interest in supporting the authority responsible for the rouble issue, which, with the development of trade with Persia and, it was now hoped, with the

Caucasus, would acquire an exchange value. The large stock of cotton, karakul (lamb-skins) and a few other commodities in hand had a substantial market value, which, with the exercise of appropriate export controls and market development, should enable the government to stablise its finances.

As the British and Indian troops in Transcaspia were maintained by the British commissariat, and considerable military supplies were being made available to the Transcaspian government without cost to them, there was at present no drain on them for foreign exchange.

This scheme was discussed with Zimen and Dmitrievsky, and while it was apparent that the Committee would have preferred a cash subsidy in a form susceptible to exchange manipulation, they indicated their willingness to accept the proposal. When it was explained that some slight delay might ensue before authorization was received from India and bullion would arrive, they demurred, pointing out that the position was daily becoming more critical.

General Malleson undertook to do everything possible to speed up authorization and the provision of silver, and urged that they should examine their own resources more closely in the meantime. It was known, for instance, that the government held a large stock of paraffin and other oil products which had been obtained from Baku and Krasnovodsk, and that there was a market for these in the Merv area as well as in Persia. This suggestion was received politely, but in private members of the Committee made no secret of their view that it was an intrusion into their domestic affairs. This attitude in the relationship between the Committee and their British allies was characteristic and gave rise to much mutual misunderstanding.

In discussing army affairs, in which General Kruten and Army Commissioner Herman took part as well as Zimen, it was clear that the Committee was anxious to obtain a clear promise of reinforcement of British troops, either from India or from Enzeli. After explaining that in existing circumstances he was unable to promise more than the maintenance of existing strength from his own resources, General Malleson informed the Committee delegates that he had hopes of obtaining a small body of infantry and artillery from Enzeli, but that the question of more substantial reinforcements would probably depend on the policy decision of the British government regarding Baku and the

Caspian area. This immediately brought up the question of British plans for that area. What are the British going to do about Baku? Would British forces from Enzeli or from Batum occupy other key points, such as Petrovsk? Would they resist a Bolshevik attempt to regain possession of these places? What were British relations with Denikin? And so on.

To all these questions Malleson was not prepared to give a definite answer, but said that he 'hazarded the guess that while Baku remained occupied, and British forces remained in the Caspian area, they would continue to exercise naval control'. He added that in the latter connection he would be raising the question of facilities for naval refit, base stores and personnel at Krasnovodsk. Enzeli, for a number of reasons, political as well as technical, was unsuitable for the purpose, whereas Krasnovodsk had machine shops, a dockyard and skilled personnel, and already formed part of the defensive scheme for Transcaspia.

Malleson was aware that the Committee would welcome any suggestion for more extensive use of Krasnovodsk, not only because of its military significance to themselves but also because it would provide a bargaining card for them to play in presenting a list of their own requirements. But for the moment Malleson contented himself with mentioning the subject as one for subsequent discussion when the whole question of British military policy had been decided.

As was expected, the question of the limitation placed on British troop movements beyond Merv was raised by the Transcaspians. They strongly urged that an effort be made to persuade the Government of India to rescind its order. The argument was presented that the recent success at Merv and withdrawal of 'Red' forces towards the Amu-Darya line was a clear indication of the weakness of the Tashkent army and command, and that a resolute advance with all forces available, if undertaken quickly before the winter set in, would be certain of success. The Committee had information that the Tashkent Soviet was having difficulties elsewhere, and that a rapid advance in force would encourage other anti-Bolshevik forces in Turkistan to move against Tashkent.

General Malleson held out no hopes that Simla's order would be rescinded. He shared the view of General Kruten that a quick follow-up of the 'Red' forces might achieve a substantial success, but he asked what steps the Transcaspian Command had taken to make the best use of the manpower and war materials they possessed. Zimen had mentioned that there was a Russian population of nearly a quarter of a million in Transcaspia. If that were so, why were so few Russians at the front? Why had better use not been made of the Turkmans? Why were domestic political matters allowed to interfere with the smooth working of the army organization?

As these questions touched on sore points—namely the lack of political unity and cohesion, not only within the Committee but among the public; failure to enforce mobilization decrees because of resistance on the part of the railwaymen and other workers; fear of the Turkmans and antagonism towards ex-officers—the Committee representatives could only reply that steps were being taken to remedy these deficiencies.

Malleson did not press the point regarding the Turkmans, but suggested that it was a matter that should be seriously considered and that the Committee might do worse than consult Turkman leaders, including Oraz Sirdar. He followed this up with the obvious remark that the problem would not settle itself: the Committee should take the initiative. He then intimated that he had proposed to visit the front-line area, with the agreement of the Committee, but thought it better to postpone this for a few weeks. He was expecting the arrival of several senior officers from India, whom he would make available to organize the command and staff of the British-Indian troops on a sound basis. The present arrangement was a compromise, which had grown out of the piecemeal posting of troops to Transcaspia, and which did not take into account the arrival of other British troops from General Dunsterville's command, with their own supply line. Moreover, he was reluctant to place any extra burden on the staff at the front at a time when reorganization was in progress following the recent operations.

A number of meetings took place at which these and other questions were discussed in greater detail. It was clear from the attitude of the Transcaspian participants that there was extreme nervousness about the internal situation, and that they placed all their hopes on receiving financial help as soon as possible. The rise in morale following the success at Dushakh had been offset by disappointment over the British standstill order which had aroused suspicion that it was a preliminary to withdrawal. Unfortunately, Malleson at this stage was unable to offer much comfort, as he felt obliged to confine himself to generalities until the situation, following the Turkish and German collapse, and the future of the British force at Enzeli, had been made clear.

In the meanwhile, however, he notified his chiefs in India regarding the Committee's acceptance in principle of the financial scheme and strongly urged that a quick decision be arrived at and that a supply of silver coin be made quickly available.[2]

Life at Ashkhabad

IN TIMES of national crisis, particularly of a revolutionary nature, a large part of the population of cities seems to be seized with a hectic desire to eat, drink and be merry—come what may. This behaviour is most noticeable among the class of people who stand to lose most by disturbance of the social order, and is probably a gesture of defiance against Fate. Even in the little Central Asian city of Ashkhabad something of this spirit was observable among the Russians whose life and prospects had been upset by revolution and civil war. Restaurants and cafés were full, and a number of establishments of the *café chantant* type did a roaring business. Ashkhabad possessed no theatre, but several cinemas continued to show old films, many of them American slap-stick comedies and French bedroom farces of the old Max Linder type.

Apart from the large number of officers at staff headquarters, a disproportionate number seemed to spend long spells of leave from the front. A certain number of ex-officers and officials of the old regime, together with their families, had taken refuge in Transcaspia before the fall of Baku; others had returned from Persia where they had betaken themselves during the previous Bolshevik regime.

The business community, largely Armenian, had money to spend, and spent it freely. Many officials, whose low salaries were a cause of complaint against the government, spent long hours in cafés engaged in interminable discussion over glasses of tea or a bottle of cheap Caucasian wine. Vodka was on sale, but was not cheap; good brandy was, however, obtainable at a reasonable price and was usually drunk in the local fashion with a lump of sugar and a slice of lemon to follow.

Entertainment was provided by a horde of young ladies who had mysteriously descended on Ashkhabad from heaven knows where. Many of these were of local vintage, pursuing their vocation in private when times were bad and facilities for public entertainment and display were limited.

Russian hospitality needs no special occasion to express itself, being limited solely by means. In Ashkhabad, at this time, there was no end to private parties; dinners, teas or simply informal gatherings to drink and gossip. Everybody talked endlessly. Any subject that came up for discussion was analysed, criticized, praised or condemned in a babble of voices, each speaker appearing to derive pleasure from the joy of argument rather than from any particular interest in the subject under discussion. Their quick intelligent Russian minds seized on any point that was raised; questioned it as a matter of course; then, like children tiring of a game, abandoned it for something else.

In their attitude towards events in their own country they often displayed a curious blend of resignation with a rather naïve sense of indignation that such things were allowed to happen. Hatred of the Bolsheviks was common, but it seemed often to be based on some personal experience of an unpleasant nature. One old gentleman would wind up a fierce denunciation of the Tashkent regime with the complaint: 'Would you believe it; they stole forty poods of sugar from my store; forty poods!'

Although Russians are generally free from snobbery, some of the ladies took pleasure in recounting, with sighs, stories of their former splendid estate, their acquaintance with Prince So-and-So and other past glories. All this was harmless, and who would have wished to deprive them in their present situation of their moments of reminiscence or fantasy?

That these friendly good-natured people had another side to their character was evident from what had been happening all around us. That ruthlessness and cruelty were not confined to the 'downtrodden workers and peasants' was shown by the behaviour of both 'Reds' and 'Whites', and the graduations in between. It was true that the workers and peasants, relieved of the restraints of the former government, of religion and of the *mystique* of Tsardom, had displayed, and were still displaying, a ferocity and callousness towards their former 'betters' that put the *jacquerie* of 1789 in the shade. In their reaction to this, 'White' officers and officials were capable of equal brutality, particularly towards Bolshevik leaders who fell into their hands. An unhappy outcome of all this was the disposition, later displayed by both sides, to put the blame for this conduct on to the 'interventionists'.

At least half the population of Ashkhabad consisted of various types of Turkmans, Uzbeks, Persians and Caucasians. A large colony of Armenians, mostly traders and workmen, occupied the densely populated quarter near the railway station and yards. The Armenians provided the bulk of the Transcaspian troops, not through any process of selection but because many Russians, being railway workers, were 'indispensable', or else were able, through Trades Union influence, to put themselves in that class and avoid being sent to the front.

It was difficult to determine what occupation, if any, was followed by the Asian community. Most of them seemed to spend their time sitting about in the native bazaars on the outskirts of the town or wandering about the streets. The Turkman was more often than not a visitor from a neighbouring *aul* or native village; some were market gardeners, coachmen or small traders in the bazaars; others belonged to the improvised cavalry units that were, nominally at least, part of the armed forces. The Russians disliked and feared these, an attitude that derived from appreciation of the fact that the Turkmans disliked Russians in general, but also from the stories of Turkman atrocities towards prisoners and stragglers.

Although outwardly there was nothing abnormal about the appearance and day-to-day life of Ashkhabad, the atmosphere of the town was tense. There was little of the feeling of common purpose among the people as a whole; various sections of the community eyed one another with suspicion or dislike; even among people who had most to lose by the fall of the government there was criticism of its members and of the administration in general. Fear or dislike of Bolshevism had been a unifying force, at least among a majority of the people; both sentiments still existed, but were overlaid by local faction, by jealousies, by fear of the Turkmans, and, among most Russians, by suspicion of the British. The Armenians who feared the Turks and Turkman tribesmen, and did not share the national pride of the Russians, were largely pro-British; the Turkmans were pro-Turk, but were not unfriendly towards the British. The Socialist-Revolutionaries distrusted the Mensheviks, and both disliked or feared the Bolsheviks. The Russian 'bourgeois' and most ex-officials and former officers despised all the socialist groups, and longed for the good old days.

.   .   .   .   .

In an atmosphere such as this it could hardly be expected that General Malleson, with his 'hard-boiled' temperament, would evince any sentimental preferences for one group or another. His attitude was determined by the task he had undertaken, and by his training as an Indian army officer to get on with his job with very little regard for the teeming life going on around him.

When not engaged in discussion with his officers, or writing despatches, he would take short drives into the hills to the south of Ashkhabad, where there was a little shooting to be had. When visitors called he would keep the interview short, leaving any details to be worked out by members of his staff. He read a good deal, mostly old-fashioned novels of the Charles Lever or Wilkie Collins type, which were sent to him from Quetta by the diplomatic bag.

He had considerable knowledge of birds and animals, and could be induced to talk freely about different species and their habits. When in an expansive mood he would also talk about such matters as the Indian Mutiny, or Kitchener's campaign in the Soudan, or the Afghan wars, on all of which subjects he was widely read. His views were frequently unorthodox and critical of authority, and even cynical. One sensed that he felt his own merits had not received due recognition, although he never permitted himself a word of criticism of his seniors in talking to junior officers. Conscientious, meticulous in small matters and hard-working, Malleson was a lonely man who could unbend only when discussing something of particular interest to himself. It is doubtful whether he found anything of interest or worthy of special sympathy in Transcaspia, unless it was the beautiful Tekke carpets, a number of which he bought or received as gifts. In the last case he invariably returned a suitable gift, usually a sporting gun or a revolver with cartridges, of which he had a collection.

Ashkhabad, although a fairly large town and the capital of the province since Skobelev's time, had little of historical interest. No earlier city had occupied its site as was the case with Merv. It had been laid out in the spacious Russian style as a military and administrative centre, its government structures being solidly built, but seldom higher than two floors. This was chiefly because of the prevalent earthquake shocks, one of which was to destroy part of the town some years later.

The cantonment and barracks were far superior in design and

structure to similar constructions in India at that time. Quarters for both officers and other ranks were excellent: bathrooms and kitchens abounded and there was a plentiful supply of hot and cold water. Parade-grounds were spacious and surrounded by trees. Any ideas that British officers in India may have entertained about the makeshift character of Russian military posts were quickly dispelled by sight of the very substantial and commodious establishments in Ashkhabad, Merv and Bairam Ali.

Throughout Transcaspia the solid and permanent character of Russian buildings was evident. The railway, running through difficult desert country, often with shifting sands, had been solidly built; its stations, goods depots, tanks and rolling stock of excellent design, the roomy passenger coaches comfortable and well appointed. There was much superficial dilapidation as a result of war-time neglect and recent disturbance, but less than might have been expected.

While it may be true, as is now asserted by Soviet writers, that the Tsarist government, and its military governors in Turkistan, did little for the native Muslim population, except indirectly, there was every sign of careful planning in public works and in such economic development schemes as had been undertaken. Irrigation, especially in connection with cotton-growing, had made considerable progress, and many of the railways and roads, completed later by the Soviet authorities, were built, or planned and surveyed, by the Imperial government.[1]

Tsarist neglect of the interests of the Kazakh, Kirghiz, Uzbek, Tadjik and Turkman population, at that time more than 90 per cent of the whole, is still the principal theme of Soviet criticism of its predecessors. The application of the term 'colonialism' in Soviet propaganda against British and other Western nations regarding their exploitation of Asian and African lands is merely an extension of its use as applied in Soviet criticism of Tsarist administration in Central Asia. The vital point which is now completely ignored in this Soviet criticism of Tsarist exploitation is the mass settlement of Russians in Turkistan, carried out extensively by former Russian governments and which, more than anything else, was responsible for the hostility, or, at best, the sullen passivity, of the native population towards their Russian overlords. Settlement of Russians and Ukrainians throughout Turkistan has increased enormously under the Soviet regime, the old free-and-easy life of the nomads and settled native villagers having been upset in the wider interests of Russian settlers, state industrialization and large-scale farming. In the long run this has brought considerable material benefits to all concerned, and has raised the productivity of the Soviet Union as a whole, but no amount of Soviet propaganda regarding their beneficent role in Central Asia can alter the fact that what the Soviet government has done, and continues to do, in this region can more accurately be described as colonialism than this term can be applied to the administrative control and development of large areas of Africa and Asia by European Powers. Except in South and East Africa, and to a limited extent in Indonesia, European settlement in Asia and Africa was on a very small scale. In Turkistan the settlement of Russians on Kazakh and Uzbek lands runs into millions, and the process continues.

In Transcaspia, a barren desert country except for the oases of Merv and Tedzhen and small fertile patches near the Persian border, there had been less economic development in Tsarist times than in the Ferghana valley and farther east and north-east. The Turkman nomads and villagers had been left pretty much to fend for themselves. Mainly nomads, living in their felt-tented *auls*, they tended their flocks, producing their sheepskins and carpets as they had done for centuries. In the oases they were small farmers and horse-dealers, living separately from the Russian population. Few of their people had any education. Their religious leaders were ignorant, and often fanatical with the narrow outlook of isolated people.

Although possessing many virtues, the Turkman had a long tradition of raiding and banditry. Once the terror of the Persian Khorasanis and the settled population of the river valleys, his raiding habits had been kept in check by the Russians. With the loosening of authority during the early days of the revolution, opportunities to exercise old habits presented themselves, and there was a certain amount of more or less organized raiding from hide-outs in the mountains or in the vicinity of the Afghan frontier. Old accounts were settled, and unpopular Russian officials and others were killed.

During the Bolshevik regime in Transcaspia the larger Turkman landowners and traders were deprived of their property, nominally in the interests of the less affluent, but really as an act of revolutionary policy, blindly undertaken and clumsily executed. As a result of this action the latent anti-Russian sentiment of the tribesmen took an anti-Bolshevik shape, so that they found themselves the reluctant and suspicious allies of the Menshevik-Socialist-Revolutionary government of Ashkhabad, and, in due course, its British collaborators.[2]

The depredations of bandits like Aziz Khan, whose services had been utilized by Oraz Sirdar during the operations near Merv, thus received some sort of official countenance. But as it was impossible to direct Aziz Khan's services into controlled channels, his services became more of a nuisance than an asset, and it was to be found necessary at a later stage to place him under restraint.

Reference has already been made to the comparative uselessness of the Turkman for cavalry reconnaisance and for planned operations. In fact, as time went on, the Turkman horsemen became a liability, as their habits of stripping and killing prisoners and stragglers, whether friend or foe, reflected on the behaviour of the Transcaspian army as a whole. Many Austro-Hungarian prisoners of war, who as a result of British post-armistice propaganda attempted to cross the desert and thus escape Bolshevik conscription, were intercepted by the Turkman cavalry and slaughtered.

It will thus be seen how complicated and diverse were the problems with which the Mission was confronted in Transcaspia as a result of the undertaking to assist the Transcaspian government. All manner of economic, political and social problems called for redress, none of which was the concern of the Mission, and which would need many years to settle. With the collapse of Turkey, and German withdrawal from the Caucasus, British military co-operation with the Ashkhabad government would lose its original justification. Meanwhile, all that could be done was to endeavour to keep the propped-up edifice intact, as far as this was possible, and await official pronouncements as to future policy.

In view of the signing of an armistice on the Western front, high-level policy decisions which would affect the role of the Mission were to be expected in the near future. The changes that had already taken place in the over-all situation were such that fresh instructions would be needed in the light of the report on the local situation that was now on its way to India and to London.

14

Sinews of War

BEFORE returning to Meshed in mid-December General Malleson took advantage of a visit by Oraz Sirdar to Ashkhabad to discuss the military situation with the Transcaspian commander. He had already consulted with the commanding officers of his own troops, now installed at Merv and Bairam Ali, pending the consolidation of a front-line position.

The Transcaspians were now entrenched at Annenkovo. Kushkh had been occupied, unfortunately too late to benefit from the store of war equipment which had been removed by the Bolsheviks. Although Annenkovo was no less exposed to a flank attack than was Dushakh, it was nearer to its supply base at Bairam Ali than the former front-line position had been to Ashkhabad. From all available information it seemed unlikely that there would be a renewal of offensive operations on a large scale by the Bolsheviks for some little time to come.

To avoid the interminable arguments which were a feature of discussions with members of the Committee, the meetings with Oraz Sirdar took place privately, only Zimen, as Foreign Minister, and General Kruten being present on behalf of the government. Captain Teague-Jones, who spoke fluent Russian, and had spent some time at the front where he had been in action with the Indian troops, was fully informed on the military as well as the local political situation, and was therefore able to prevent the meetings being taken up with side-issues.

Oraz Sirdar made no secret of the fact that he was greatly disheartened by the order from Simla restricting the movement of British troops to defensive operations. He seemed to have little confidence in the ability of his own forces to make a further advance unaided by British and Indian troops, but at the same time he urged the desirability of moving forward to the Oxus before the winter set in. He regarded the Annenkovo position as untenable in the event of a renewal of the offensive by Tashkent, and doubted the ability of his troops, about whose fighting capacity and morale he had no illusions, to stand up to a resolute attack unless substantially reinforced.

Both Oraz Sirdar and General Kruten continued to urge that General Malleson should endeavour to persuade his own chiefs to permit the British-Indian contingent to participate in an advance to Chardzhou. While they had hopes of securing the services of some Caucasian cavalry from General Denikin and perhaps a few officers and specialist Russian volunteers from Baku, these, they thought, were hardly likely to arrive before the end of December.

Oraz Sirdar raised the question of Bukhara. As members of the Committee had already suggested, the Emir of Bukhara had a large, if poorly equipped, army at his disposal, and considered himself to be threatened by the Bolshevik government at Tashkent. He was less likely to enter into an agreement with the Transcaspian government than with the British, and while his troops could hardly be expected to play any part in operations in Transcaspia, it was in his interests to co-operate with an anti-Tashkent force to free Chardzhou, which was in his territory.

General Malleson was unable to hold out any hopes to Oraz Sirdar that the Indian government order would be rescinded, but reassured him that there was no immediate intention, so far as he was aware, of withdrawing forces from Merv. Some reinforcements could be expected from Krasnovodsk, and he hoped to provide more guns and perhaps aircraft in the near future. As regards Bukhara, Malleson urged Oraz Sirdar to ascertain what were the Emir's views on the situation, and his intentions towards Tashkent, but added that the Emir was not to be led to suppose that British co-operation would necessarily be forthcoming.

During the course of these talks Zimen intimated that he had hopes of obtaining assistance from General Bicharakov, now back in Baku. Bicharakov was engaged in the setting up of a Central Caucasian government together with a group of politicians whose past record did not inspire much confidence in their ability to win popular support. It was no secret to members of the Malleson Mission that Zimen had been in correspondence with members of this group and that he had been angling for some form of agreement with them. As it was uncertain what

Bicharakov and his new colleagues were aiming at, Malleson held the view that no fresh commitment was desirable, at any rate until the still-confused political situation had been resolved in Baku.[1] Moreover, so long as British troops were in Transcaspia it was essential that Krasnovodsk should remain under their control and continue to function as a transit point and base for any naval operations that might have to be undertaken in the event of a Russian Soviet naval attack from Astrakhan.

Therefore, while not discouraging Zimen from seeking reinforcements and supplies from the Caucasus, Malleson reminded him that the agreement with the Transcaspian government provided for British utilization of the port and installations at Krasnovodsk for the period of hostilities. Malleson, therefore, wished to be assured that no political agreement which might affect the position at Krasnovodsk would be entered into with a third party without the agreement of the British Mission. Slightly dashed by this blunt speaking, Zimen hastened to assure Malleson that no arrangement had been made or was contemplated, but made the quite reasonable point that the limitations placed by the Government of India on the movements of Malleson's own troops, and the changed situation following the Turkish collapse, must of necessity compel the Transcaspian government to seek additional help where it could find it.

Malleson's decision to return to Meshed for a few weeks before visiting the front was occasioned by the arrival there of his army commanding officer, Brigadier-General Beatty, with several staff officers. General Beatty had been serving with Indian army forces in France and Egypt, and until his present appointment had commanded the cavalry brigade at Lucknow. Brigadier-General Dickson, Inspector of Communications of the East Persian Cordon, was also expected in Meshed, where a conference was to take place before Beatty left for the front to take over his command.

Another urgent requirement was the arrangement for the issue of the promissory notes and the disposal of the silver currency, part of which would be brought by Beatty's party. Consultation with a representative of the Imperial Bank of Persia was necessary for the implementation of the scheme to be adopted.

Before leaving Ashkhabad, Malleson had a confidential talk with

Dorrer at the latter's request. Dorrer, who was in an agitated state, said he was gravely disturbed about the internal situation in Transcaspia. Bolshevik propaganda, and agitation by the underground Bolshevik organization, was not without effect, and he felt doubtful whether the Committee as a whole had the support of more than a section of the population. Its fear of the Turkman made it hesitant to give the tribesmen more arms, and while there was no fear that they would exchange their support of the Transcaspian government for allegiance to Tashkent, they might try to take control of the country into their own hands if and when the British left.

Dorrer, who was evidently trying to obtain more definite information about British intentions than Malleson had been able to give Zimen, went on to say that he expected trouble in Ashkhabad in the near future. Railwaymen, town workers and public servants were restive and coming under the influence of agitators. It was only because of the vigilance of Drushkin's police that matters had not yet come to a head.

Asked whether the opposition elements preferred the Tashkent regime to that of the Transcaspian government, Dorrer replied that he thought the majority did not; they had supported the revolt against Frolov and his gang, but there was a strong feeling against the 'White' Russian regimes of Kolchak and Denikin, who were popularly regarded as aiming at a return of the old regime. The mass of the workers were less pro-Bolshevik than anti-'White'; some of them resented our presence as being reputedly supporters of reactionary generals and capitalists.

Dorrer went on to say that members of the Committee were by no means united in their political attitudes. There was no longer any idea of trying to reach an understanding with Tashkent; that had been considered at the outset, but it was now too late. Even if the Tashkent Soviet were disposed to talk it would be on their own terms. From his knowledge of the leading personalities in Tashkent he thought that several of them would agree to discussions, but he had no doubts what the outcome would be, and he, for one, would wish to have no part in it.

With this warning in mind, Malleson and his staff returned to Meshed on December 19th, Malleson having instructed his representative in Ashkhabad to keep a close watch on the situation and report any developments that were indicative of a worsening of the position as indicated by Dorrer.

Authority having been received from India to proceed with the financial plan, the Committee was informed that financial assistance was forthcoming and the suggestion was made that in anticipation of this help an increase in the wages of the railwaymen and officials should be granted at once. In this way it was hoped that one source of grievance would be removed and opposition to the government lessened.

The Committee evidently preferred to wait until the British promissory notes were in circulation before acting on this advice, although promises were made of early wage adjustments. The immediate crisis had been averted, and helped by the arrival in Ashkhabad of the 28th Cavalry and the Warwicks, the Committee was able to keep the situation in Ashkhabad temporarily under control, although it was clear from all available information that opposition was deep-seated and too widespread to be dispelled by palliative measures.

The necessary promissory note forms had been printed, and a small 'Finance Section' formed to supervise and control the issue. Two finance officers were sent to Ashkhabad to undertake these arrangements. The Committee had already published a notification in the Ashkhabad Press explaining the nature of the note issue and its relation with their own currency arrangements. In order to strengthen public confidence in Transcaspia, in the issue and in the Committee's own financial measures, a plan was devised whereby the silver currency brought from India, or obtained through the Imperial Bank of Persia, would be unloaded, weighed and counted in the presence of witnesses. In this way it was hoped that the new currency issue would obtain popular acceptance from the start.

In reporting to the Government of India on his views of the situation in Transcaspia, Malleson was far from optimistic about the ability of the Committee to remain long in power without British support, and pointed out that troops, as well as members of the Mission located in Ashkhabad and elsewhere, were precariously situated. He considered that support of the Transcaspian government, financially and otherwise, should continue as long as British troops remained in the country, and that whatever the ultimate decision might be it should be borne in mind that the lives and property of many thousands of

The Bukharan Envoy and General Beatty

White Russian reinforcements to Transcaspia from the Caucasus, 1919

The British Consulate at Meshed in winter

The garrison church at Ashkhabad

The road between Meshed and Ashkhabad

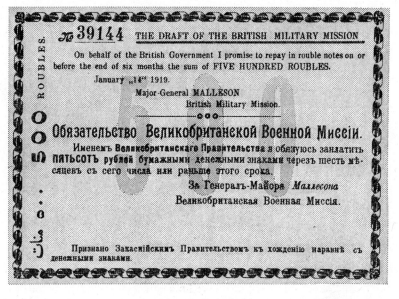

№ 39144   THE DRAFT OF THE BRITISH MILITARY MISSION

On behalf of the British Government I promise to repay in rouble notes on or before the end of six months the sum of FIVE HUNDRED ROUBLES.

January „14ᵗʰ 1919.

Major-General MALLESON
British Military Mission.

— o o o —

Обязательство Великобританской Военной Миссіи.

Именемъ Великобританскаго Правительства я обязуюсь заплатить ПЯТЬСОТЪ рублей бумажными денежными знаками черезъ шесть мѣсяцевъ съ сего числа или раньше этого срока.

За Генералъ-Майора *Маллесона*
Великобританская Военная Миссія.

Признано Закаспійскимъ Правительствомъ къ хожденію наравнѣ съ денежными знаками.

Fig. 2. *Above:* A reproduction of a genuine promissory note as issued by the Malleson Mission
Below: A spurious note, produced in Ashkhabad after the departure of the Malleson Mission. Note errors in spelling

№ 6247   THE DRAFT OF THE BRITISH MILITARY MISSION.

On behalf of the British Govermnent J promise to pay 3 months after of date to bearer the shm of FIVE HUNDRED ROUBLES.

Desember „ *12* ....." 1918.

Mojor General
British Military Mission.

Обязательство Великобританской Военной Миссіи.

Именемъ Великобританскаго Правительства я обязуюсь заплатить черезъ три мѣсяца съ сего числа предъявителю сего ПЯТЬСОТЪ рублей

Генералъ-майоръ *Маллесонъ*.

Великобританская Военная Миссія.

Признано Закаспійскимъ Правительствомъ къ хожденію наравне съ денежными знаками.

people would be in jeopardy if there were to be a too-hasty withdrawal or if the government were to collapse.

Brigadier-General Beatty, together with two staff officers, Major Thompson and Captain Ibbotson, were already in Meshed. They had made the journey from Quetta in less than a week, a speeding up of transportation that had been made possible by completion of repair work on the road carried out by the sappers and levies under General Dickson's command.[2]

Beatty, a large jovial man, exuding energy and good fellowship, took the measure of his new chief at once, adjusting himself to Malleson's withdrawn personality with evident ease. Although temperamentally poles apart, they had a common interest in wild life and in shooting which manifested itself in excursions into the neighbouring countryside. With little interest in the ideological questions and political problems with which the Transcaspian situation was beset, Beatty regarded his role clearly and simply as a military one. To take over the command of troops which were precluded by orders from advancing, even when the enemy retired after an unsuccessful attack, could hardly be regarded as an attractive prospect, and one that would need all Beatty's tact and ability. As it was still uncertain what new orders would be forthcoming, or what the future role of British troops would be in the light of events elsewhere, all plans had to be of a provisional nature. With uncertain allies, and the possibility of a collapse in the rear, precautionary steps for eventual retirement over the Persian border had to be taken, without these becoming known to the public or rumours of a British withdrawal reaching Tashkent.

The question of providing some reinforcement for Malleson in east Persia had been discussed with Beatty before he left India, but he had been given to understand that any decision about the sending of additional troops would depend on developments in Afghanistan and the North-West Frontier of India and on the outcome of policy talks then proceeding between the government of India and the British government. In any case, if any temporary reinforcement of Malleson's troops in Transcaspia was to be provided, it would in all probability come from the British force in Baku or from the Black Sea army in occupation of Constantinople and Batum.

It had been intended that General Beatty and his staff should proceed to Bairam Ali in December, but in view of the exchange of telegrams between Simla, London and army staffs regarding moves and changes in area commands, General Malleson decided to keep them in Meshed until the position became clearer.

The formation of an All-Russian government at Omsk by Kolchak, and the successes achieved by Denikin's forces in south Russia and the north Caucasus, suggested that a Bolshevik collapse was within the realm of possibility. The future of anti-Bolshevik regimes, such as the Transcaspian Committee, thus seemed to depend on the outcome of civil-war operations elsewhere, and in particular on the struggle then at its height between 'White' and 'Red' in Siberia, the Ukraine and in north Russia. With the cessation of hostilities in Europe, and the collapse of Turko-German plans in the East, the role of missions and detachments of troops in north Persia and Transcaspia could hardly remain unchanged for long. A return to peaceful conditions seemed unlikely in the foreseeable future; all the forces unleashed by revolution and civil war, and the unreconcilable outlook of 'Reds' and 'Whites,' precluded any possibility of agreement between the various parties, groups and national sections being attained by negotiation. One side or the other must win and impose its authority on the rest. In the prevailing atmosphere in Europe, still conditioned by the stresses and sharp judgements of war, the hopes of the majority of people were placed on the side of the 'Whites', who, it was generally considered, represented the forces of law and order and normality. As time was to show, this was a simplification of a complex issue, but the stresses and strains of four years of war, and the shock of violent revolution in Russia with its new leaders preaching revolt and disorder, had produced an emotional state of mind in which judgements could hardly be expected to be based on objective and balanced criteria.

Although public opinion in the West, as a whole, had been sympathetic towards the Russian revolution, the excesses of Bolshevism and the violence of the Communist propaganda attack against the former allies of Russia alienated even that section of the community that favoured non-interference in Russian affairs.

Intervention, despite reaction against Communism, was, however, generally unpopular, and as the earlier progress of 'White' armies turned to failure and disaster, their leaders displaying no understanding of the revolutionary mood of the Russian people, the demand for the withdrawal of Allied missions and troops became general in Western Europe and America.

In remote Meshed little was heard of these developments, but it was clear that, with the changed situation, withdrawal from advanced and, in certain cases, untenable positions was only a question of time.

15

After the Turkish Capitulation

BRITISH troops from 'Norperforce' at Enzeli, now back in Baku, and Captain Norris's naval force, both under General Thompson's command and reinforced by the addition of several more armed ships with British officers and Russian crews, were keeping a close watch for possible raids by Soviet ships based on Guriev and Astrakhan. General Thompson's chief responsibility was to enforce the terms of the armistice on the Turks, whose troops were still encamped outside Baku and along the railway to Elizavetpol. The Turkish commander, Nuri Pasha, on the curious pretext that a large part of his mixed force were under the command of the Azerbaijan government, showed little disposition to withdraw his army. The Turks had looted Baku and were in possession of their ill-gotten gains; they also held as prisoners a number of prominent non-Muslim citizens whom they had been 'squeezing' to compel them to disgorge their wealth.

Much damage had been done to the oil and harbour installations during the Turkish occupation. It was considered essential to get these repaired, and the oil pipe-line working with the least possible delay. The economic life of Baku was at a standstill; food was short and the currency situation confused. Many thousands of unfortunate Armenians had been slaughtered by the Azerbaijani 'Tartars'. Unless a firm hand was applied the racial conflict would continue, with disastrous results for all.

The new Baku government, mainly Azerbaijani, was a provisional one, and therefore unrepresentative of the varied groups of the population. General Thompson, as head of the occupying force, had therefore the delicate task of maintaining law and order, rebuilding public administration and enforcing the departure of the Turks, while encouraging the creation of as representative a form of government as was possible in the circumstances.[1]

Troops from the British Salonika army were shortly expected to arrive in Batum from Constantinople, but there was still some uncertainty regarding the relationship between those troops and the Menshevik government of Georgia. The Germans had departed in haste through the Ukraine, but in the North Caucasus and the Kuban region the 'White' armies of Generals Krasnov, Denikin and others were in conflict with the rapidly growing 'Red' armies. Their relations with the 'independent' Georgians, Armenians and Azerbaijanis were strained, as they did not recognize the new status of the Transcaucasian states.

The naval base had been shifted from Enzeli to Krasnovodsk, where a small garrison of British troops had taken over responsibility for the defence of the port. Although this arrangement had been accepted by the Ashkhabad Committee, it had given rise to a certain amount of ill-feeling, and was interpreted by many as indicative of British intentions to establish themselves more or less permanently in the area.

To the east of the front line, in Bolshevik-held Turkistan, mobilization of all able-bodied Russians was in progress, and a thorough reorganization of the command and equipment of the 'Red' Army was taking place. The Turkistan Republican Government in Tashkent was faced with famine conditions throughout the steppe area and at the same time had to contend with a now widespread revolt of the Muslim population as well as with a revival of the counter-revolutionary activity of the 'White' so-called Turkistan Military Organization. This movement, controlled by an underground organization in Tashkent, was widespread, but little was known regarding its ramifications, or of its leadership. Its leaders seemed to have based their plans on successes by the various 'White' armies, particularly that of Admiral Kolchak in Siberia, and may have taken into account the possibility of a British advance from Merv to the Oxus. British contacts with certain of its agents, entered into for Intelligence purposes, have been interpreted and deliberately exaggerated by Soviet historians as attesting British political support for these activities, and even direction of 'White' plans. Even the 'Alash' revolt in Kazakh territory, which followed closely upon the Kokand incident, and which for a time was associated with Admiral Kolchak's forces in western Siberia, is attributed by Soviet historians to foreign, and chiefly British, influence. That rebellion, like the Basmachi revolt, was triggered off by the repressive measures taken against the Kazakhs by a new Russian regime that was as fully determined as its Tsarist predecessors to keep power in Russian hands, and to obtain possession of Kazakh lands for Russian settlement. This it achieved by force of arms.

With the withdrawal of the Bolsheviks from the Merv area, opportunities for obtaining intelligence from Tashkent and other centres beyond the Oxus were seriously reduced. Other channels were gradually opened, but information now took some time to reach Meshed. Some information of doubtful reliability was obtained from prisoners and from Austro-Hungarian refugees, who, with great risk to themselves, crossed the desert and gave themselves up. The Austro-Hungarian war prisoners, who had been enrolled in the 'Red' Army, surrendered to the British-Indian troops in large numbers, and were then transported to Krasnovodsk for evacuation to the Caucasus and eventual return to their homelands.[2]

Malmiss was well informed of the activities of Bolshevik agents in north Persia and in Afghanistan. Several weeks previously three Soviet emissaries from Tashkent arrived in Persia by way of Sarakhs and announced that they had been sent on an official mission from the Turkistan government to discuss the cessation of hostilities. The three Russians, Babushkin, Afanasiev and Kalashnikov, had no credentials and appeared to have no precise instructions as to their mission. They were placed under arrest in Meshed pending inquiries regarding their antecedents and positions in Tashkent. Kalashnikov, who announced that he was an ex-officer and opposed to the regime in Tashkent, whose service he had entered in order to escape from the country, had met Colonel Bailey in Tashkent and confirmed the latter's presence there. The other two appeared to be sincere adherents of the Tashkent regime, but were critical of its policies and behaviour towards members of other socialist parties.

In response to a notification to India of the arrival of the three men in Meshed, Malleson was instructed to hold them as hostages for the safety of Colonel Bailey and the American Consul Tredwell and other British and American citizens in Soviet hands. On being informed by a member of the Mission of this intention, Kalashnikov asked to be permitted to send a radio message to Tashkent with a request that he and his colleagues be exchanged for Bailey and other British citizens held in Turkistan. A message to this effect was sent, but no reply was received, probably because the Cheka in Tashkent was unable to lay hands on Bailey, who was in hiding.

Eventually Babushkin and Afanasiev were sent to India to be held as hostages. Kalashnikov, having announced that he wished to place his services at the disposal of the Ashkhabad government, was sent to Ashkhabad. On his arrival there he was promptly arrested on the orders of the Committee, and evidence having been produced at his subsequent trial that he had taken an active part in repressive measures against non-Bolshevik elements in Tashkent and in propaganda against the Transcaspian government, the court sentenced him to death and the Transcaspians shot him. Such were the depths to which revolutionary and counter-revolutionary leaders had sunk through fear and mutual hatred.

It was no secret that agents from Tashkent were attempting to stir up trouble in Afghanistan, and that the ambitious clique of mullahs and tribal politicians at Jelalabad, who eventually killed the Emir and seized power, were in touch with agitators in Tashkent. The character of those who were responsible for the Emir's assassination was shown by their subsequent behaviour, and by the conflicting nature of the intrigues that were unfolding at Kabul. While seeking Soviet aid, the Afghan plotters sought contacts with anti-Soviet Basmachi forces in Turkistan; while asking Tashkent for help, they were considering giving help to the Emir of Bukhara; and in declaring their friendly intentions in relation to the Soviets, they plotted for the retrocession to Afghanistan of the Tedzhen oasis area which had been seized by Russia in 1885, an event which had nearly led to war between Great Britain and Russia.

Such a situation provided Malleson with many opportunities for creating confusion in the enemy camps by disclosing through appropriate channels to each side information as to what the other side was secretly aiming at. During the Afghan war, which was to break out early in the new year after the murder of the Emir Habibullah, full scope was given to opportunities for conducting a form of 'political warfare' and deception, presented by the duplicity of both parties. This was to give rise to many legends regarding the British role in the confused situation that had arisen, most of which will undoubtedly

The 28th Indian Cavalry

Russian staff officers and a
British liaison officer

The sole reconnaissance aircraft
used by the Transcaspian officers

Soviet stamps issued December 1st, 1933, to commemorate the fifteenth anniversary of the death of the Twenty-six Commissars: Shaumian (*upper left*), Dzhapadze (*upper right*), the Commissars lined up for the shooting (*lower left*), and the memorial building near Krasnovodsk.

The Cheka in the Caucasus in 1919; the banner reads 'Extraordinary Commission (Cheka), death to the enemies of the proletariat!'

remain current until unbiased historians have access to original records and can separate facts from propaganda.

The prospect of a British conflict with Afghanistan was disturbing, although General Malleson, who had a unique knowledge of the Afghans, was firmly of the opinion that any adventure undertaken by politicians in Kabul would not necessarily be followed by similar action in Herat and Kandahar. Precautionary steps were taken along the East Persian Cordon line, and rumours of the impending arrival of a large British-Indian force in east Persia were spread in the bazaars of western Afghanistan. The Hazaras, numerous in that area, were known to be friendly, several thousand of them being in British service as road and transport workers.

In Khorasan the situation was quiet, the 'Caucasian Committee', stunned by events in the Caucasus and the Turkish collapse, confining their efforts to the spreading of rumours about alleged atrocities on the part of the British in the Muslim holy places. As there was little sympathy among Persians for Afghans, no trouble was anticipated from that quarter.

While the food situation throughout Persia was still bad, it had eased since the previous winter, when famine had devastated many areas of northern and western Persia. The Mission had provided a large quantity of food for local distribution, which was undertaken by the army to avoid the dishonest diversion of supplies which invariably attends relief work in Eastern countries when conducted through local agents.

The complete indifference displayed by some Persian landlords and officials and affluent citizens to the distress of the less fortunate was a striking contrast with their more attractive qualities. One of the most gifted and, in some ways, most civilized of peoples, the Persians seemed at that time to lack social conscience. Indifference to the sufferings of animals is all too common in Eastern countries and Persia was no exception to the rule. Horses were well cared for, but the little beast of burden, the patient donkey, was ruthlessly exploited and overworked. While Persian poetry is full of references to nightingales and other singing birds, no interest seemed to be taken in bird-life, other than shooting those that were edible. The almost universal signs of decay and poverty that characterized the country in those days were indicative of the apathy and deterioration of public morale that had been brought about by misgovernment, and of the sad condition to which a once great civilization had fallen. Foreign occupation was undoubtedly partly to blame, but the chief responsibility for the existing state of affairs seemed to lie elsewhere. Fortunately, a change has come over the country since those days, largely due to the energy of one man, Riza Khan, and an able successor, but also to American and British help and the financial benefits which Persia has derived from the exploitation of the oil resources in the Gulf area.

By this time members of the Mission had established friendly relations with several Persian officials. Although the presence in Meshed of British troops was no more welcome than occupation by the Russians had been, they were shown much courtesy by Persian officials. Persian houses, so uninviting from the outside, were bright and pleasant once one had penetrated the forbidding wall that separated them from the narrow dusty street. Visitors would be invited to sit on beautiful rugs and wine and fruit would be brought. Conversation was usually conducted in French and ranged over many topics, but seldom touched on politics or the motives for the presence of the British in Persia. These brief interludes did something to compensate for the monotony of daily life in a city that had little to offer outside official duties.

As a holy city, Meshed was the burial place of many thousands of pilgrims, the bodies of the dead being brought from far-distant places for interment in the vicinity of the great mosque. Yet an air of neglect and indifference enveloped these dusty graveyards, the larger tombs falling into the decay that appeared to have overcome most buildings in the town, including the smaller mosques and *medressehs*.

With the oncoming of winter, Meshed lost any charm that the presence of trees and vegetation gave the city. The dusty streets became muddy tracks, and the great Maidan an expanse of slush and pools of dirty water. The smell of burning camel-dung pervaded the town. The wretched beggars stood in the shelter of the mud walls shivering in the cold and wailing their appeal to passers-by.

In the absence of precise instructions from India, Malleson decided to return to Ashkhabad and notified G.H.Q. in India accordingly. In acknowledging his telegram outlining the situation, earlier instructions concerning the stand-still of Malleson's troops in Transcaspia were reaffirmed, with the suggestion that they should be stationed for the time being near the Persian frontier. It was further intimated that the question of Malmiss and the force coming under the command of General Milne was under consideration.

As the suggestion that the troops in Transcaspia should be quartered near the Persian frontier was an indication that neither G.H.Q. nor the political authorities in India had a clear grasp of the situation in Transcaspia or of the physical conditions of the region, Malleson decided that his best hopes lay in an early meeting with representatives of General Milne's command who were already on their way to Transcaspia from Constantinople. Malleson therefore replied that he proposed to visit the front with General Beatty to examine the position on the spot, and would report his findings and make his recommendations in due course.

It was at this juncture that news was received from Ashkhabad of a renewal of the internal crisis. Having surmounted the first serious display of opposition to their rule, the Committee had been unable to stabilize their position and were once more faced with a situation that was beyond their unaided capacity to handle.

16

Crisis in Transcaspia

THE crisis, which had been brewing for several weeks, was brought to a head with the government announcement that the mobilization of all men between the ages of twenty-one and twenty-five was to be undertaken. All the efforts of the Committee to obtain volunteers from the workships, railways and factories had failed. The number of Russians at the front, apart from ex-officers and a few soldiers from the former Tsarist garrison forces and the withdrawn Persian expedition (Baratov's army), had been steadily diminishing, the railway workers in particular resisting all efforts to persuade them to enlist for active service. Thus, the very element in the population that had resisted the decree of Tashkent to mobilize manpower now resisted and even actively sabotaged the attempt by the Transcaspian Committee to conscript a single age group.

The activities of Bolshevik secret agents, and of members of the Bolshevik underground organization, had increased since the re-opening of communications with Baku. The financial crisis, now on the way to being overcome, but still acute, and the rising cost of living were not the only factors in popular dissatisfaction. The railway workers who held a whip-hand over the government in a roadless country dependent on the working of the railway line for its existence as well as for supplying the front, kept up a constant pressure on the government, their demands for higher wages and other concessions being used by their militant leaders, now more often than not secret Bolshevik agents, to whip up political agitation and resistance to government orders.

Other factors were fear of counter-revolution and dislike of the 'White' generals, distrust of the Turkmans and a not unnatural dislike of the presence of foreign troops on Russian soil.

Several hundred Daghistani cavalry belonging to Bicharakov's cavalry force had been brought to Transcaspia as a result of Zimen's negotiations with the provisional government in Azerbaijan. These troops, on arrival in Ashkhabad, proceeded to create disturbances by looting the bazaars and by riding around the streets at full speed and generally making a nuisance of themselves. Instead of entraining them without delay for the front, the Committee injudiciously kept them in barracks in Ashkhabad, evidently considering that their presence there would add to the security of the government. This action had exactly the opposite effect.

On December 30th and 31st a number of meetings of railway and other workers were held in Ashkhabad and other centres. Called for the ostensible purpose of discussing the workers' own problems and presenting demands for higher wages, these meetings quickly took on a political character, pro-Bolshevik spokesmen demanding negotiations with the Bolsheviks, the opening of the front and finally the expulsion of the British.

Immediate action was taken by the Committee to ban meetings and a number of arrests were made. The Daghistanis were sent to the front, together with a number of other troops who had been undertaking guard duties. This threw the responsibility for maintaining order in Ashkhabad on the British.

The Committee then announced that unless a considerable sum of money was made available at short notice to satisfy the railway workers' demands its members would have no alternative but to resign. These tactics were obviously designed to force Malleson's hand. It was clear that the British commander could not tolerate chaos at the rear while his troops remained at the front. What was not so clear to the Committee was that the British authorities in London and India were becoming increasingly opposed to deeper involvement in the domestic affairs of Transcaspia now that the war was over, and that the resignation of the Committee, unless followed by the formation of a new government with the same objectives in view, would absolve the Mission from providing any further assistance.[1]

After twenty-four hours of negotiation they reaffirmed their intention of resigning. The suggestion was made by Teague-Jones on behalf of Malleson that Zimen should attempt to form an alternative government. This he declined to do, but later declared his willingness to serve in a reconstituted committee with increased powers, provided further financial help from the British was forthcoming. The resignation of the Committee took place on January 1st, but it remained in office until the morning of the 3rd, when it was replaced by a new committee calling itself the 'Committee of Public Safety', consisting of Byelov as Chairman, Zimen as Foreign Minister, Drushkin as Minister for Public Security and Hadji Murat representing the Turkman population. General Kruten retained his post as military adviser in an *ex officio* capacity. Although no very clear legal basis existed for this move, it seemed to be the only alternative to chaos. The new Committee was therefore assured of British support. The former Turkman representative, Obez Baev, took command of Turkman cavalry at the front.

An order was issued by the Committee on January 1st and reaffirmed on the 4th, forbidding all public meetings until further notice. This was followed by the imposition of censorship on all external correspondence to control propaganda activity directed from Baku and elsewhere in the Caucasus. In issuing these orders the British Mission was cited as jointly responsible for enforcing the first, while the public was allowed to assume that the censorship order had, at least, the blessing of the British. It is perhaps questionable whether this implicit association of the name of the British Mission with the change of government and the first public acts of the government should have been permitted. At that time it was doubtless regarded as unavoidable and perhaps as necessary. Its ultimate effect was to saddle the British with responsibility for enforcement of law and order, and to create the legend that the new Transcaspian government was little more than the puppet of the British Command, a viewpoint that has received official sanction in all Soviet accounts of the Transcaspian episode.

An immediate issue of a further batch of British promissory notes helped to ease the financial strain. Notwithstanding the clear statement in the text of these notes, and in the public announcement concerning their issue, that payment would be made in roubles after ninety days, there was a widespread impression that payment would be made in some other currency, even in bullion; some hoarding of the notes kept them out of circulation. This was to give rise, at a later date, to entirely unjustified charges of chicanery. Some notes even found their way abroad, and were being presented to mystified bankers and exchange brokers. This was to lead to further recrimination, and even to the charge that the whole operation was a financial swindle, a charge that no objective inquiry could sustain.

While these domestic complications were being unravelled, General Malleson received notification that direction of the Mission and the troops in Transcaspia had been transferred from the Government of India to the British War Office and that they would henceforth be locally responsible to General Milne. In anticipation of such a move, preliminary steps to substitute the Krasnovodsk–Baku supply line for the Meshed–Birjand–Quetta line had already been taken, an additional reason for taking firm steps to ensure the smooth and uninterrupted working of the Central Asian railway.

General Beatty took over the command of the British-Indian troops at Merv and Bairam Ali during the first week of January. As news was being received of a concentration of Bolshevik troops at Chardzhou and Ravnina, he immediately entered into consultation with Oraz Sirdar's staff for organization of the line of defence. It was assumed that the attack, when it came, would be a heavy one and that an attempt would be made to outflank the Transcaspian position. Cavalry patrols were sent along the line and north and north-east of the Annenkovo station. Captured prisoners confirmed the main plan of attack, which included demolition of the railway line in the rear of the Transcaspian position.

The attack started in the early morning of January 16th. It had been a bitterly cold night, and a thick mist covered the desert, making observation difficult but also providing cover for the movement of troops by each side. In spite of precautions taken to protect the railway, enemy demolition parties succeeded in blowing up a section of the line in the rear of the armoured train at Annenkovo, but by 10 a.m. a repair party succeeded in making good the damage, by which time reinforcements from Bairam Ali were in position, and cavalry screens were well out in the desert on either flank. By 11 a.m. the main body of the enemy was reported advancing behind an armoured train about three miles from the Annenkovo front line. The train opened fire with its two guns, but the shells went wide or passed well over the front line, the fog preventing the gunners from estimating the correct range. At the same time a large enemy force was reported advancing from the north-east covered by artillery fire. Turkman and Caucasian cavalry sent out to intercept this advance fell back quickly in the face of heavy fire. In the meantime the main body pressed home the attack, while the enemy flanking movement had reached the rear of the Transcaspian armoured trains.

At this moment a company of the 19th Punjabis arrived from Bairam Ali, and immediately went into action, driving the enemy force right back across the original Transcaspian line which had been abandoned. The 28th Cavalry and a large force of Turkman horsemen then attacked the enveloping Bolshevik line, driving their troops, who seemed to have lost contact in the fog, back in confusion. A further frontal attack on the Transcaspian armoured train was defeated by a determined counter-attack by the whole of the train-crew and the Russian and Armenian infantry protecting it.

The Bolsheviks thereupon began a general retirement. Seven machine-guns were captured, but the enemy was able to withdraw all his artillery. His losses were more than 500 killed and wounded and many prisoners. The losses on the Transcaspian side were less than half this number, including twelve killed and thirty-six wounded of the 19th Punjabis and two or three of the 28th Cavalry wounded.

From prisoners it was discovered that the total enemy force had been brought up to nearly 10,000 of which 1,500 were former prisoners of war. Twenty trains of troops had been brought up to Ravnina, as well as eight field guns and a large number of machine-guns. Rations had been issued for a three-day operation, which was to include an encircling move from the north and a drive through the Transcaspian position to Merv.[2]

Exactly why the Bolsheviks broke off the attack it is difficult to judge. Staff plans seemed to have gone awry, and the fog made lateral contact difficult. But their preponderance of military strength, their heavier artillery and tactical advantage in attack should have enabled them to sweep aside the Transcaspian defence. Once again their command failed them or their planning was defective. Their troops fought bravely, as is attested by their heavy casualties. On the Transcaspian side all units fought well, which disposed of the contention of the railwaymen's leaders at Ashkhabad that the troops at the front were only waiting an opportunity to lay down their arms. Even the Turkman cavalry obeyed orders, and after the earlier retirement rallied and drove the flanking force of Bolshevik troops back in panic. After this engagement a combined effort could easily have driven the Bol-shevik army back to the Oxus. But this was not possible without the co-operation of British and Indian troops, and the opportunity was lost.

No further move was made by either side, the front remaining static until after the British had withdrawn at the end of March, when the Bolsheviks, heavily reinforced by Soviet troops brought by rail from central Russia via Orenburg, which had already been recaptured from Dutov, attacked the Transcaspians and drove them back to Merv.

The legend, which Soviet historians have created, to the effect that the 'Red' Army drove a British army, several thousand strong, pell-mell out of Turkistan, is thus on a par with Soviet accounts of the Basmachi revolt. The Soviet account of these events completely distorts the picture of events in Turkistan in 1918–19, and provides a convenient back-ground for the current version of the re-establishment of Russian authority in Central Asia. By grossly exaggerating the number of British troops in Persia and Transcaspia; by falsifying dates; and by imputing motives that are entirely fanciful, and charging the British with possessing plans for the permanent occupation of Turkistan, Soviet historians, following the party line, seek to find justification for the actions of the revolutionary leaders of 1918–19, and interpret their conduct as necessary measures to deal with foreign-supported counter-revolution and British 'imperialism'.

17

Winter Stalemate

WHEN Malleson set up his headquarters in Ashkhabad again during the second week of January the town was outwardly quiet, the presence of a half-company of the Warwicks from Krasnovodsk and a squadron of the 28th Cavalry ensuring that no plot to overturn the government or to sabotage supply arrangements had any chance of success. Although reluctant to interfere in the domestic affairs of the Committee, Malleson had no intention of permitting any flagrant breach of public security while troops under his command remained at the front. That this would alienate still further that section of the community that was opposed to the presence of British troops disturbed him not in the least, as held he no brief for any group or party, regarding all with equal distaste. At the same time he regarded himself as committed to the support of the government, within the terms of the agreement, and so long as a British force remained in the country.

The new Committee's financial measures were now in operation. The first supply of silver coin received from India was in the hands of the bank, and preparation for the new note issue were well advanced. A quantity of roubles had been purchased in Persia and had been made available to the government as an advance in anticipation of future arrangements, and some payments for supplies and other services had been made in Persian *krans* to relieve the exchange situation.

There had been some patrol activity at the front and intermittent shelling from armoured trains by both sides, but otherwise all was quiet. Rumours of large Bolshevik concentrations at Chardzhou were current, but all available information suggested that no large-scale attack from that quarter was to be expected at an early date. German and Hungarian ex-prisoners of war captured during recent operations reported that mobilization of all available manpower was in progress, but that the war prisoners were no longer displaying willingness to fight in the Bolshevik ranks. Several thousand of these had been enrolled, some as volunteers, but the majority with one object in view, namely to break through the one obstacle to repatriation, which they supposed was the front at Annenkovo. Only distorted news of the end of the war in the West was reaching them, the local newspapers reporting highly coloured accounts of revolution in Austria and Germany and revolutionary disturbances elsewhere.

As a British force was now at Batum and was moving along the railway towards Tiflis, an early visit by representatives of General Milne's 'Black Sea' Command was shortly to be expected. The decision to undertake the occupation of Transcaucasia pending a decision as to the future of the Transcaucasian state had been reached at the forthcoming Peace Conference had been taken by the War Cabinet in London in mid-November, although evidently without any clear idea as to what was to be done about it. At that time the main objects appear to have been to withhold oil supplies from the 'Red' armies and prevent the infection of Bolshevism extending into Persia and the Middle East. The future of areas such as Armenia and Georgia, which had proclaimed their independence and were clamouring for Allied recognition, was likely to come up for discussion at the forthcoming Peace Conference at Versailles and much lobbying by various interested parties in London, Washington and Paris had already begun.[1]

The main body of the British-Indian force was at Bairam Ali, twenty miles east of Merv, and at the front-line position at Annenkovo, some fifty miles north-east of the latter place. The British troops at the front were regarded as being on outpost duty, and were in fact regularly relieved by other sections of their own units at Bairam Ali. At that time the whole British force consisted of one company of the 1/4th Hampshires, ninety strong, three squadrons of the 28th Cavalry, three companies of the 19th Punjabis and one battery of the 44th Royal Field Artillery. (At Ashkhabad were stationed one squadron of the 28th Cavalry, one company of the 19th Punjabis and two companies of the Royal Warwicks.) The total strength of this force was therefore well under 1,000 men. Transcaspian strength was about twice this number, including the Turkman cavalry units, and was shortly afterwards increased to about 2,500 by Daghistani Cossacks and a few infantry and artillerymen from Denikin's forces in the Caucasus.[2]

Merv (since renamed Mari) was at that time a smaller, but less solidly built edition of Ashkhabad. Standing in an irrigation area, its immediate surroundings were relatively well cultivated and the streets of the town itself were tree-lined, with many gardens and orchards. Although comparatively few Transcaspian troops were stationed in the town, the streets and cafés were full of Russian officers and their wives. As in Ashkhabad, numerous Turkman and other native central Asian types were to be seen about the streets, while the bazaar, an open one, might have been that of any small town across the border in Khorasan.

The Merv oasis is the larger of the two great irrigated areas in the eastern part of Transcaspia. It is watered by the Murgab river, which rises in the Parapomisus range in the extreme north-west of Afghanistan. After flowing through 200 miles of semi-desert country it splits up into the numerous channels which irrigate the oasis, and then flowing northward peters out in the sandy waste of the Karakum. The ancient city of Merv, once a great centre of civilization, lies in the extreme eastern part of the oasis, close to the modern Bairam Ali. Little remains of the old city but battered ruins and numerous mounds.

To the north, the Karakum, the Black Desert, stretches to the swamps at the southern end of the Aral Sea, the area surrounding the old walled city of Khiva, and eastward to the Amu-Darya, the 'mighty Oxus' of history and legend. The desert is virtually impassible, except by the few caravan tracks running north and south, which link up the infrequent and brackish wells.

The whole Tedzhen–Merv area has been the scene of many historical events and has seen the passing of the Turki and Mongol hordes which devastated Persia and neighbouring countries in the Middle Ages. The native Turkman population are a remnant of the Turkish tribes that moved westward and formed the great Ikhan dynasty on the ruins of the Bagdad Caliphate, and later the Ottoman Empire of modern Turkey.

The various tribes of Turki-speaking peoples of Turkistan—the Uzbeks, Kazakhs, Kirghiz and Turkman peoples—are interrelated, although there are Mongol and Persian strains. The Tadjiks are partly of Persian origin and still speak a form of the Persian language. The Turkman population in and around Merv had suffered from repression during the Bolshevik occupation, and were disposed to take their revenge on Russians in general—'Red' or 'White'. Although many of them were serving in Oraz Sirdar's cavalry, it could not be said that there was any enthusiasm for the Transcaspian government's cause. They were regarded as dangerous and unreliable by all Russians.

Bairam Ali town was little more than a village surrounding the railway station, but at a short distance, a beautifully laid out park and plantation encompassed a small palace and a group of official buildings. The palace had been built as a shooting-box for the late Tsar, but was never used by him, although other members of the Romanov family visited it. It was now occupied by the British headquarters staff.

The whole area, which is well watered and covered with a thick growth of grass, shrubbery and various kinds of native and exotic trees, was alive with game, including pheasants, partridges and snipe. In the adjacent oasis along the Murgab and Tedzhen rivers a species of tiger was to be found, as well as other kinds of wild life.

During staff talks with the Transcaspian Command an opportunity was provided for extended talks with Oraz Sirdar and members of his staff. The commander of the Transcaspian forces was a short thick-set man of about sixty, with a pleasant bearded face, keen eyes and the bowed legs of a horseman. He had been educated at the famous Corps de Pages in St. Petersburg, probably in chivalrous recognition of his father's exploits at Geok Tepe, and had then served in Kornilov's 'Savage Division', a cavalry corps made up of Caucasians and Turkman tribesmen. (Until 1916 the native population of Turkistan were not liable for military service, but Turkman horsemen from the Tekke tribe served in cavalry units as volunteers, some of their leaders, such as Oraz Sirdar and Obez Baev, holding commissioned rank.)

Oraz Sirdar still aimed at advancing to the Oxus before the Bolshevik forces had had time to regroup their shattered army. He counted on Dutov holding the Orenburg line and Kolchak continuing to advance from his Siberian base. He also maintained contact with Bukhara, and appeared to entertain a higher opinion of the military capacity of the Emir's troops than his own Russian chief of staff, who considered the Bukharans of little more value than a threat to the Tashkent flank and a 'container' of 'Red' troops.

The apparent inability of the Transcaspian Committee to raise more troops was causing Oraz Sirdar deep concern. Neither he nor his chief of staff had much confidence in the politicians at Ashkhabad, whom they regarded as being both timid and unrealistic, and distrustful of their own officers as well as the Turkman. Oraz had succeeded in increasing the number of Turkman cavalry to 1,500 and by more careful selection of officers, and training in the use of machine-guns, had improved their quality as troops. Given more equipment and a free hand to recruit, the Transcaspian commander considered he could form a Turkman Division, but the Ashkhabad authorities evidently wished to keep the Turkman numbers down to about 50 per cent of the total force.

Oraz Sirdar once more made his plea for British participation in an advance to Chardzhou, even hinting in an indirect way that a British military government of Transcaspia might not be a bad thing, a suggestion that had been put to our chief liaison officer in Transcaspia on several occasions by Turkman leaders in Ashkhabad. Once again Malleson had to explain that his hands were tied by his orders, and that while he had every sympathy with Oraz Sirdar's needs, he could do little more than help him to hold the Merv area and provide equipment and training. He explained the arrangements for General Beatty's appointment and asked Oraz for his views on adjustments in command organization.

It was clear from Oraz Sirdar's reply that he would have been glad to hand over the command to General Beatty, but, as that was obviously impossible, he merely remarked that he foresaw no difficulties. He and Beatty would be able to work together, and he welcomed his appointment. In the meanwhile he was strengthening the position at Annenkovo, where he hoped to stage a flanking attack on the advanced line of enemy armoured trains in the near future.

18

Envoy from Bukhara ·

APART from the protection from enemy observation that was afforded to the armoured trains by sand-dunes, it was difficult to see what advantages Annenkovo offered as a front-line position. The desert on both sides of the railway was flat and featureless, except for occasional ridges of sand and small clumps of the stunted plant, *saxaul*, the only source of fuel in the desert region.

The armoured trains were drawn up in line in the shelter of the sand-dunes, a loop line having been constructed along the single line of track to allow each train to return to Bairam Ali for refuelling and to transport reliefs to the front. The Transcaspian troops lived in the trains, maintaining outpost positions about half a mile in advance of the leading train. Gun-pits had been constructed on slightly elevated positions on the flanks, and a line of picket posts and shallow trenches extended on each side of the railway for several hundred yards into the desert. These were wired, but the only protection against outflanking were similar earthworks a little farther out and towards the rear. These were occupied by day, but in the now bitter cold of the night the pickets were apt to return to the shelter of the trains.

A company of the Punjabis lived in felt *kibitkas* close to the trains and shared the outpost duties. They were regularly relieved from Bairam Ali. Cavalry patrols, also accommodated in *kibitkas* on the left flank of the main position, made daily reconnaissance excursions into the desert and in the direction of Ravnina, some six miles distant, where the 'Red' outpost was situated. These patrols had occasional clashes with 'Red' calvary, each side avoiding a general engagement, while the 'Reds', with their longer-range guns, from time to time sent over a few shells, which usually fell wide of the Transcaspian position.

On December 7th Oraz Sirdar sent a larger force to probe the enemy's position. Both sides spent a good deal of ammunition, the

Bolsheviks making no attempt to counter-attack, to the quite evident relief of the occupants of the armoured trains and troop trains, who could only with difficulty be persuaded to leave their stuffy and unhealthy quarters.

As at Kaakha, the most reliable element in the Transcaspian force were Russian officers and non-commissioned officers who manned the artillery, and the Meshed-trained machine-gun unit. They performed their duties without thought for their physical comfort, and were a striking contrast to the Armenian and Tekke infantry. A railway repair unit and demolition section also consisted of Russians and performed excellent work under Russian engineer officers.

A thin layer of snow covered the desert and icicles hung from the roofs of the trains. A keen wind blew continuously, bringing the temperature down to zero at night. Apart from the trains, which were cold and uncomfortable, the only real shelter was afforded by the round felt *kibitkas*, which could be quickly erected and dismantled. These were the normal habitation of the nomad Turkman from time immemorial, and are in fact mentioned by Marco Polo, who traversed the region nearly 700 years ago.

Similar conditions prevailed at Ravnina, except that the Bolsheviks did not possess the advantage of a base close to their rear. A support position was held at Uch-Adzhi, some twenty miles back, but their trains had a 100-mile journey to make to refuel at Chardzhou. Their great problem was fuel, their locomotives having been adapted to use *saxaul* and even dried fish from the Aral Sea. Their own stocks of oil were nearly exhausted, supply from the north being completely blocked by Dutov's troops at Orenburg.

In telegraphing his preliminary report to India, Malleson urged that the troops under his command should remain at Bairam Ali and Merv pending further orders, and that no attempt be made to take up quarters elsewhere. He pointed out the disastrous effect of a withdrawal from the advanced position that such a move would have on Transcaspian morale, and that furthermore no winter shelter existed away from the Merv area.

In the meantime Zimen had again been in touch with the provisional government at Baku, to whom he had proposed an alliance, and had made arrangements for a further detachment of Bicharakov's troops to be sent to the Transcaspian front to reinforce the Transcaspian army.

. . . .

During a visit to Bairam Ali by General Malleson and his staff the question of Aziz Khan's activities came up for discussion. In existing circumstances Malleson was reluctant to criticize any arrangements made by Oraz Sirdar to strengthen his own force, but the activities of Aziz Khan and his band of desperadoes, set in motion by Oraz Sirdar for military purposes, were now seen to serve no practical end. Aziz was out for loot, and to enhance his own position as a 'khan'. Instead of raiding enemy positions and cutting the railway, he had been raiding villages in the oasis area, showing no discrimination in choosing his victims.

Oraz Sirdar listened attentively to Malleson's remarks and admitted sadly that Aziz had failed him. He undertook to issue a warning to Aziz, and even to take steps to have him arrested and his gang dispersed unless he confined his efforts to military objectives.

Oraz Sirdar once more brought up the question of co-operation with Bukhara. He again set forth his argument for reaching an understanding with the Emir, urging the strategic advantage of a threat to the Bolshevik railway communications, and the reaction that an attack by the Emir's army on the Tashkent army would have on the Uzbek and Kirghiz population of Turkistan, already in a state of revolt against Tashkent.

In reply, Malleson urged restraint. Apart from the fact that he was insufficiently well informed about the state of the Emir's forces, he considered that it was a matter that should first of all be considered by the Ashkhabad Committee, and in any case he had no evidence that the Emir was, in fact, ready or willing to undertake such action. Thereupon Oraz Sirdar produced what he evidently considered as his trump card. An envoy of the Emir of Bukhara was at this moment in Bairam Ali and was anxious to meet General Malleson.

Malleson could hardly decline to meet the envoy without offending Oraz Sirdar, so therefore agreed to meet him that evening. In reality, Malleson was both interested and pleased to have the opportunity of meeting the envoy of a state in which nineteenth-century Indian army officers had shown so much interest, with tragic results for those two members of his own corps, Colonel Stoddart and Captain Connolly, as previously mentioned. In any event, Malleson hoped to be able to clarify a situation regarding which the Ashkhabad Committee had always been very reticent. It was clear that the Committee, while welcoming help from any quarter, were reluctant to enter into any firm agreement with Bukhara, as they suspected that some form of collusion with the Turkmans would be the inevitable outcome. Like Malleson, they welcomed the existence of the potential threat to Tashkent but hesitated to encourage the Emir to commit himself to hostile action against the Bolshevik regime in Turkistan. Malleson's hesitancy was based on uncertainty as to the length of the British stay in Transcaspia and the existing 'stand-still' order for British-Indian troops; that of the Ashkhabad Committee was due to their distrust of the Turkmans, and the ingrained Russian intention to remain the top dog. (A similar situation existed in Tashkent, where the Soviet government retained the traditional Russian attitude towards the native population, an attitude that was to be castigated later by Stalin himself in his report on 'Nationalities and the Colonial Question' at the 10th Congress of the Communist Party, as an example of 'Russian Great Power Chauvinism'.)[1]

The Bukharan envoy, an impressive old gentleman, with a henna-stained beard, attired in a magnificent silken robe, was duly produced. After an exchange of courtesies, in which Malleson excelled himself to the astonishment of his aides, the conversation was continued in the privacy of the railway coach that was being used as a travelling headquarters. The Bukharan envoy understood Russian but preferred to speak Persian, so that the conference was conducted in three languages. This slowed down the proceedings somewhat, and strained the ingenuity of the interpreters in finding equivalent terms for the language of honorifics used on both sides.

From this conversation it appeared that the Emir had no proposition to make but was seeking information and advice. Did the British intend to take Chardzhou or even advance on Tashkent? If so, what was their attitude towards Bukhara? The Emir had heard, with admiration, of the exploits of the Indian soldiers: could instructors be made available for his own army? What were General Malleson's views of the situation as a whole?

General Malleson explained as tactfully as he could that the British were in Transcaspia to assist the Transcaspian government and not to undertake military or political action independently of their agreement with the Transcaspians. He was certain that his own government entertained the most friendly feelings towards the government and people of Bukhara. The present situation was very confused, but there were rays of hope that it would become clearer in the near future.

In reply to the envoy's remark that the Emir would be glad to have any advice that General Malleson cared to offer him, Malleson replied that he strongly advised caution. A false step might be dangerous; it would be better to wait until the whole internal Russian situation became clearer.

The envoy then asked if General Malleson's own government would be willing to provide him with modern weapons, of which he was short. He would also welcome having instructors in their use. Malleson replied that he would give the matter his full consideration, and in the meantime he sent his good wishes and friendly greetings to the Emir. With this, and a further exchange of courtesies, and an exchange of gifts, Malleson took his leave. (The Emir sent Malleson a pair of Bukharan carpets and a silken robe; Malleson sent him a pair of handsome sporting rifles with cartridges, which he carried with him on the off-chance of being faced with a situation of this kind.)

In response to his report to India on this meeting, General Malleson's attitude was approved, and he was granted permission, *at his own discretion*, to make available to the Emir a small quantity of rifles and ammunition, if these could be spared.

Oraz Sirdar made no sign of his disappointment that nothing more concrete had emerged from the meeting. He evidently regarded the conversation as a first step, and, as an Asian, could appreciate that in the Orient negotiations took time and were invariably preceded by a sort of diplomatic sparring and discussion on generalities.

On his return to Ashkhabad on the following day, Malleson prepared and sent off to India detailed reports of his visit and his impressions. He again drew attention to the desirability of avoiding any immediate action that would place the Ashkhabad government in an embarrassing situation, alienate the Turkman leaders and which, at the same time, would upset the financial and other arrangements which were just beginning to bear fruit.

Several days after Malleson's return to Ashkhabad an advance party consisting of two senior officers from General Milne's staff arrived. One of these, Colonel Carleton, made a quick visit to the front accompanied by a member of Malleson's staff, while the other made a survey of the military arrangements in Ashkhabad. Arrangements were now complete to effect the transfer of control of British military forces in Transcaspia from India to the War Office, so that Malmiss would henceforth be responsible to General Milne, now in command of the newly formed 'Army of the Black Sea'.

A series of conferences now took place during which all aspects of the local situation were ventilated. Members of the Committee were encouraged to express their views and put forward suggestions. Zimen, evidently suspicious of the ultimate outcome of these deliberations, pressed for more substantial help and a clear statement of policy. As matters stood, with a considerable proportion of the Transcaspian Russian population neutral if not hostile, the Committee was obliged to envisage the gradual inclusion of their territory within the orbit of the 'White' armies of General Denikin unless the British came forward with a clear policy of continued support. Thus the Committee, secretly suspicious of both the British and Denikin, was dependent on one or the other, a state of affairs which most of them were unable to face with equanimity.

Again they were asked what they were doing to make the best use of their own resources, and again they evaded the question by pointing out their financial and other economic difficulties, and the complex character of their domestic situation.

On the 21st of January, General Milne himself, accompanied by several members of his staff, arrived in Ashkhabad from the Caucasus. After a short visit to the front and discussions with General Beatty and unit commanders, Russian and British, they spent a few days at Ashkhabad and Krasnovodsk, then returned to Baku. Several days later Malleson was informed of the decision to withdraw all British and Indian troops from Transcaspia, and was requested to report without delay as to the earliest date on which this difficult task could be accomplished.

19

Decision to Withdraw

THE decision to place the Mission and the British troops in Transcaspia under General Milne's command, although not unexpected, was considered unlikely to take place so soon after General Milne's visit. The change of command was welcomed by all members of the Mission, including General Malleson himself, who for some time past had noticed an extraordinary lack of interest in the work of the Mission on the part of his chiefs in India. No visit had been made to Meshed or the front by any representative of the Political Department or army headquarters in India. Supplies had been made available and demands for funds met, but only after considerable delays. Very little guidance had been given, and that only in a negative sense, rather suggesting that the authorities had no clear ideas on the subject or were preoccupied with important matters closer at hand.

Far from projecting a 'plan to seize and colonize Turkistan' or urging Malleson to act with that object in view (as Soviet historians would have their readers believe) the Government of India provided Malleson with the vaguest of instructions, limited the sphere of action of the troops under his command and displayed the utmost reluctance to be drawn into any commitment that involved expenditure or the provision of manpower. Once the Turko-German threat had vanished, the interest of the authorities in India, never profound, faded out.

The task with which the Malmiss force was now faced was the difficult one of disengagement. It was obvious that this could not be undertaken at once; much diplomacy and tact would be needed, and in all fairness to the Transcaspians they would have to be given an opportunity to secure alternative support and help in bridging over the transition period.[1]

The first communications from India on this subject suggested an early withdrawal, and completely ignored the difficulties and risks that this would entail. As Malleson felt it would be fruitless to enter into a discussion with India on this point, he submitted his recommendations to General Milne and the War Office for a delay of four to six weeks, urging that existing supply arrangements to the Transcaspians be continued for the time being, and that surplus military stores be handed over to Oraz Sirdar's command when the evacuation finally took place. Apart from other considerations, time was needed to pay off the outstanding promissory notes.

General Milne showed a clear understanding of the problems involved and gave Malleson authority to make his own arrangements for withdrawal by stages or in a single move, as he thought fit, postponing the date line until the end of March. British troops were to be evacuated via Krasnovodsk, and all Indian troops were to return to north-east Persia to be reincorporated into the East Persian Cordon or withdrawn to India.

Armed with these instructions, Malleson decided that the intention to withdraw must be kept secret for the time being, informing only Beatty and his immediate entourage, the commander of the East Persian Cordon troops and General Dickson. In the meantime holders of the promissory notes were to be encouraged to accept repayment before maturity. Direct payments to the Committee for services and local supplies were henceforth to be made in coin or Persian currency.

Steps were taken to evacuate all sick and wounded on the grounds that adequate facilities for their care now existed at Baku, and that hospital ships were now calling at Batum. No additional stores for our troops, other than essential replacements and day-to-day needs, were brought into the country.

Rumours were spread through behind the enemy line that the British were preparing a plan to attack the Bolsheviks via Bukhara and by a wide detour below Chardzhou, crossing the Oxus at a lower point and linking the armed Turkman troops with insurgents operating farther east. These rumours, which were 'substantiated' by the planting on Bolshevik agents of specially prepared documents, evidently had the desired effect, as Intelligence reports soon indicated that the Bolsheviks were making preparations for a further retreat at the first sign of an attack.

(Some of these fabricated rumours have become the 'facts' of Soviet historians, judging by the very confused accounts of military operations given in personal reminiscences of these strenuous days by retired officers of the 'Red' Army, published in Central Asian journals and newspapers.)

The timing of the decision to withdraw may well have been influenced by the steps being taken by the British government to hasten the demobilization of national forces and reduce expenditure. Lloyd George was at that time engaged in an effort to wind up war-time ventures in the Caucasus, the Caspian area and elsewhere, and was urging on his colleagues that an effort be made to bring together the leaders of the 'Red' and 'White' forces in Russia and the various political groups to examine the possibilities of peace by mutual agreement. This led to the abortive Prinkipo proposal for a conference between all parties, which was to founder on the refusal of the 'White' generals to take part in talks with the Bolsheviks and distrust by the Allied leaders of the Soviet's declared aims.

These facts were not known to the Mission at the time, although the proposal for a meeting on the Island of Prinkipo in the Sea of Marmora was made public towards the end of January. The immediate problem was to extricate the British and Indian troops with the least possible disturbance of the situation in Transcaspia, while retaining such contacts throughout the area as would enable the Mission to keep Simla and London informed of the development which must inevitably follow our withdrawal. The threatening situation in Afghanistan, Bolshevik machinations in that country and in Persia, and the activities of revolutionary agitators operating from Tashkent against the British in India, could all be watched more easily from Meshed and other key points in Persia than from Ashkhabad.

At this time two Indian revolutionary agitators, Mahendra Pratap and Barkatullah, were in Tashkent, where they were known to be working in close association with the local Soviet. Pratap had spent the war years in Berlin and Turkey, and after the German capitulation had gone to Afghanistan via Petrograd, where he had been in consultation with Lenin. In Kabul he endeavoured to persuade the Emir Habibullah to abandon his policy of neutrality and break with Britain, but without success. He then turned to the Afghan opposition elements who were plotting against the Emir, and who were deeply engaged in a conspiracy with tribal leaders on the North-West Frontier of India and members of the so-called Caliphat party in the Punjab to promote disorder in northern India.[2]

Mahendra Pratap designated himself head of a 'Provisional Government of India' which he had formed with German support in Berlin, and had appointed Barkatullah as his Foreign Minister. When in Kabul, Pratap had been closely associated with a Turkish officer, Muhammed Kazim Beg, who had been a member of a Turko-German Mission to Afghanistan under von Niedermeyer, a German diplomat. Having failed in their mission to bring Afghanistan into the war against the British in India, they turned to the opposition party, providing its leaders with advice and money.

The activities of the opposition groups in Afghanistan and their links with Tashkent, as well as with subversive elements in Peshawar and Lahore, were well known to the Government of India. What was not clearly known was the connection between these activities and the Soviet government in Moscow. Propaganda and intrigue conducted by the regime in Tashkent seemed to accord with pronouncements from Moscow, but the manner in which these were conducted suggested the hand of the enthusiastic amateur, making mischief without any clear idea of the ultimate object to be attained.

The internal situation in Tashkent, according to Intelligence reports, was unsettled. A revolt had taken place against the Soviet regime, instigated by an ex-officer, Osipov, who had thrown in his lot with the Tashkent Bolsheviks and held the important post of War Commissar in their service. After an initial success the rising had been crushed by 'Red' Guards, and a wholesale and indiscriminate massacre of several thousand of the bourgeois population had followed. This uprising, which seems to have been badly organized, may have been linked with the activities of the 'White' counter-revolutionary organization in Turkistan or may have been a domestic affair. In Soviet accounts it is asserted, without any evidence to substantiate the allegation, that the revolt was instigated by 'British imperialists', the ubiquitous Colonel Bailey being charged with complicity in the affair. As, according to his own account of his sojourn in Turkistan, Bailey at that time was in hiding in a distant village nursing a broken leg, this seems most unlikely; nor is it reasonable to suppose that members of a revolutionary regime in conflict with a rebellious native population and threatened on two fronts would risk their necks by shooting each other at the behest of a British agent.

The revolt failed, and much disorder and bloodshed ensued. Osipov and some of his companions escaped, and are alleged to have joined 'White' forces operating in Siberia; according to one account they found their way to Bukhara, but nothing further was heard of them.[3]

The revolt in Tashkent, following hard upon the failure at Annenkovo, resulted in a series of impassioned appeals by the Tashkent Soviet to the Soviet government in Moscow, all recorded by Malmiss's radio service. Shortly afterwards Soviet troops from Tsaritsin (later Stalingrad, now Volgograd) attacked Dutov's force at Orenburg, supported by a simultaneous attack from the south by troops from Tashkent, with the result that Orenburg was captured on January 24th, thus opening up communications with Russia and bringing relief to the beleaguered Turkistan Bolsheviks. Trained agitators and Communist officials accompanied the 'Red' Army, with instructions to take over the administration from the feeble hands of local party men, and to embark on a campaign against British imperialism in Asia. Support was also to be given to revolutionary elements in Afghanistan and Persia.[4]

In the light of these developments, which presaged an early resumption of the offensive by the Tashkent Bolsheviks, now reinforced by new leaders, troops and equipment from Russia, Malleson decided that members of the Committee must be informed in confidence of the British decision to withdraw. Only by doing so could he secure their co-operation when the time came; moreover, they should be given time and opportunity to secure assistance from the Caucasus and take precautionary steps to prevent a rising by opposition elements in their own area.

After consideration of the risks involved it was decided as a first step to inform General Kruten in strict confidence and obtain his views. An honest man, although not blessed with outstanding military qualities, General Kruten was known to have no political affiliations and to be able to keep his own counsel. He was thereupon told of the intention to withdraw our troops by the end of March. He evinced no surprise, taking the news calmly. He informed Malleson that he was already engaged on a plan to obtain troops and war material from Denikin, but was hampered by lack of funds and secure means of communication with Denikin's representatives in the north Caucasus.

Kruten was encouraged to go ahead with his plans and if possible to visit Baku and Petrovsk personally. He was told that the necessary funds would be made available and that he would be given whatever facilities he might need in Baku or Petrovsk, or wherever he might find it convenient to contact Denikin's representatives. It was agreed with Kruten, however, that the Committee should be informed of the position, and their authorization for such a move should be sought. This was done on the following evening, February 4th.

As was to be expected, the news caused great consternation. Although members of the Committee could not fail to have anticipated the possibility of such a move, they had been buoyed up by the hope that the change of command on the British side might result in agreement to co-operate in an advance on Chardzhou. Without indulging in reproaches (these were to come later), they asked what the British proposed to continue doing to assist them in their task, which they had always considered to be a common effort. They were told that promised supplies that had not yet been delivered would be made available, and that a considerable quantity of military stores held by the British force in Transcaspia would be placed at their disposal. Malleson said he foresaw the possibility of some further financial arrangement but could not commit himself at that moment. Promissory notes would be redeemed, and facilities for obtaining oil and other supplies from Baku would be extended.

The proposal for sending General Kruten to the Caucasus was then raised, Malleson repeating his offer to provide the necessary funds and to facilitate the journey. This was agreed, and arrangements were made for Kruten to leave without delay.

Although nothing was said during the discussions on the subject of the Turkman troops whose loyalty to the Transcaspian government had been influenced by British regard for their interests, both Hadji Murat and Oraz Sirdar (who had been brought to Ashkhabad for the meeting) later raised the question of continued support for the Turkmans. In private they presented an earnest plea for some kind of declaration of British interest in the Turkman tribes. It was explained that for political, geographical and military reasons no such proposal could be entertained, and it was urged that they continue to give their support to the

Committee as offering the only hope for the achievement of at least some part of their aims.

The Committee allowed no hint of these proceedings to reach the public. In keeping their counsel, they were, of course, acting in their own interests. The immediate effect of the disclosure to the Committee was to increase the authority of Drushkin, the most energetic member of the government and the one responsible for public security.

Zimen took the decision deeply to heart, and at leisure was to find time to produce a number of legal arguments suggesting that there was no time limit to Malleson's obligations, and that these could not be determined unilaterally. While Malleson could sympathize with this attitude, the niceties of legal argument had little bearing on the case, as the conditions in which the agreement had been reached had changed, the chain of command had been altered and in Transcaspia the existing government enjoyed nothing like the same measure of public support that had been accorded to its predecessor at the outset.

Although the decision to withdraw was a matter of high policy, and inevitable sooner or later, it was not possible for members of the Mission to withhold a feeling of self-reproach for the abandonment of people for which they had acquired sympathy and understanding. Not normally affected by sentimental considerations, Malleson shared this feeling, and in his report to India he again drew attention to the plight of the Committee and to the sad lot of many who had worked loyally with the British Mission and who stood to suffer from its withdrawal. He urged that he be authorized to provide help in cases of hardship, that food and other supplies belonging to General Beatty's force should be handed over to Ashkhabad when withdrawal took place and that recognition be given to officers and men in the Transcaspian army who had given outstanding service. This was agreed.

Those who felt themselves to be heavily compromised through their close association with the British Mission and the British-Indian force were given assistance to enable them to transfer themselves and their families to places of safety. A number of former officials took advantage of this offer and made their way to the Caucasus or to Constantinople and Egypt. Few officers availed themselves of this offer, but remained with the Transcaspian forces until their defeat by Frunze's 'Red' Army some months later.

20

Rearguard Action

THE Ashkhabad 'Committee of Public Safety' was now definitely linked with the 'White' counter-revolutionary front. What had started as a revolt by Menshevik and Social-Revolutionary workmen against a short-sighted and doctrinaire Bolshevik government at Tashkent had now, with the turn of events, become an ill-sorted combination of non-party Russians and Turkman tribal leaders fighting for their very existence. Dependent in the first instance on British help to escape destruction at the hands of a revengeful Tashkent army, they were now becoming part of the 'White' volunteer army organization in the Caucasus. More than half their troops were Turkman; their officers were 'White' ex-regulars, and such local support as they now enjoyed was mainly that of the middle class and of that section of the workers who, because of their association with work of the Committee, could expect only short shrift from the Bolsheviks if captured.

Together with several other active Social-Revolutionary ex-members of the former government and administration, Funtikov was arrested by Drushkin on a charge of plotting against the new government. The exact nature of the charge was not made public, and it seems unlikely, in view of the role he played at the time of the Ashkhabad and Kizyl Arvat revolts against Taskhent, that he was plotting to establish relations with the Bolsheviks. These arrests were probably precautionary measures taken by the new Committee in the light of the events in Ashkhabad at the end of December.

The new Committee for all practical purposes was a dictatorship, but it is difficult to see how any administration could have functioned otherwise in the circumstances. Their only hope lay in maintaining the front intact and safeguarding the rear, while linking up with 'White' movements elsewhere, which at that time were making headway against the Bolsheviks.

At the front the situation remained quiet. Throughout the month of February no action was undertaken by either side. Patrols made their regular excursions into the desert, now deep in snow, but the main body of the Transcaspian forces and the British and Indian troops kept to the shelter of their trains or their winter quarters at Bairam Ali. As had been expected, the Daghistani Cossacks had been difficult to handle, becoming restless and undisciplined and a nuisance to the townspeople.

Towards the end of February small bodies of troops began to arrive from the Caucasus. These reinforcements came from Denikin's army, which was now operating in the north Caucasus and had occupied Derbent and Petrovsk. Many ex-officers of the Russian army who had been in hiding, or had otherwise managed to survive in Baku, joined Denikin; some of these were sent to Transcaspia. By the beginning of March several hundred infantry and artillery troops had arrived at Bairam Ali from Petrovsk, and more were expected. One of Denikin's senior officers, General Lazarev, was sent to Ashkhabad to take over the command and bring the staff organization into line with that of the volunteer army.

During the first week of March news of the impending British withdrawal was made public. This immediately evoked appeals from all classes of the community for delay, the Turkman people especially submitting further pleas for British protection. Once it became clear to all that the decision to withdraw was irrevocable, many people left Transcaspia for Baku or elsewhere in the Caucasus, or made preparations to do so.

Several senior officials of the government resigned, including Dorrer; two Ministers followed a little later. Byelov was the first to go, the post of Chairman being taken by Zimen. Byelov was followed by Drushkin, who left for the Caucasus in March, when there was a regular exodus of prominent anti-Bolshevik personalities who had evidently lost confidence in the ability of the regime to survive.

The lively atmosphere that had prevailed in Ashkhabad in the autumn months had changed to one of apathy. The snow-covered streets were still full of apparently aimless people, soldiers and Turkmans predominating. Carriages of the two-horses *drozhky* type were largely replaced by sledges whose tinkling bells enlivened the otherwise silent streets. The temperature frequently dropped to zero, but the calm days which followed the high winds of December and January, and long periods of sunshine, made the cold tolerable.

The only activity at Annenkovo was the daily patrol, carried out in turn by the 28th Cavalry, the Daghistanis and the Turkmans. Contact with the enemy took place on March 2nd when a patrol of the 28th Cavalry was intercepted by a 'Red' cavalry force of more than twice their number. A fierce struggle ensued, in which the men of the 28th, using both lance and rifle, drove off the enemy patrol, losing only two of their number, who were taken prisoner. (Both of these men subsequently escaped and found their way back to their comrades in Meshed, a feat for which they were both decorated.) This was to be the last engagement in which the British-Indian troops were to be involved before the retirement into Persia took place on April 1st.

Part of the British force was withdrawn early in March when troops from Denikin's army began to arrive at the front. Arrangements were made for all the Indian troops to leave the front towards the end of the month, some via Muhammedabad, but the majority via Ashkhabad and Kuchan. Most of the British troops had been withdrawn to Krasnovodsk, where a British naval base was to remain for several months. Most of these men were evacuated to Batum via Baku and Tiflis, to be transported to England for demobilization.

The promised rifles and a small quantity of ammunition had been sent to Bukhara by camel-train in February. The caravan was accompanied by two Indian N.C.O.s, but no official emissary was sent to Bukhara by Malleson. In many Soviet accounts reference is made to British officers and instructors having been sent to Bukhara by Malleson. No British personnel, other than the two Indians, went to Bukhara. Soviet accounts of British officers having been sent to Bukhara and Khiva are entirely fictitious, and are evidently intended to provide a plausible explanation for Muslim hostility towards the Bolshevik regime in 1918 and 1919.

When sending the rifles Malleson wrote to the Emir in friendly terms but once again urged him to refrain from any action that might provoke retaliation by Tashkent. Malleson was fully aware of exchanges between the Bukharan and the Afghan governments and the efforts of the Emir of Bukhara to obtain help from Kabul; also that opposition leaders in Kabul were in touch with the Soviet government in Tashkent, as well as with Indian agitators there. The revolt in Jelalabad near Kabul, which took place on March 21st during which the Emir

Habibullah was assassinated, and which was a precursor to the Anglo-Afghan war, was a factor in determining the decision to hasten the withdrawal of the Indian troops into Persia, where they were needed to protect the line of communication and guard the personnel of British bases and supply depots in Meshed, Birjand and in Seistan.[1]

Several members of the Mission staff had been withdrawn to India in February and March or had been transferred elsewhere. Teague-Jones, whose tact and diplomacy in dealing with the Committee had been invaluable, and who had been responsible for ensuring the continued support of the Turkman leaders to the Ashkhabad government at a time when the Turkish advance into Transcaspia seemed imminent, returned to his own branch of the service. His close association with the Ashkhabad Committee from the beginning of the British link with that body has led Soviet historians of the time and place to identify Teague-Jones's name with all acts of the Committee, a convenient assumption which is entirely unjustified and unsupported by evidence. This attitude on the part of Soviet writers is, however, fully in line with the attempt to saddle the British and Americans with responsibility for provoking internal opposition to the Bolshevik regime in Turkistan at that time, and to explain away embarrassing events arising out of early Bolshevik mismanagement and intolerance by attributing to foreign intrigue the inevitable outcome of their own actions.

During March all promissory notes that were presented were paid off, but unfortunately forgeries soon appeared; a number of these found their way to Baku and elsewhere in the Caucasus, where their holders demanded payment in British or some other staple currency. See illustration p. 117. This gave rise to some correspondence with General Thompson's staff in Baku, in consequence of which two members of Malleson's staff went to Baku at the end of May to assist in settling this and other difficulties that had arisen as a result of the British withdrawal into Persia.

As the final day of the withdrawal drew near, difficulties arose with the Committee in regard to the provision of rolling stock to transport troops from Merv. This trouble was not due to any ill-will on the part of the Committee but to sabotage by members of the Railwaymen's Union. As negotiations seemed to be fruitless, recourse was had to the time-honoured procedure of the Middle Eastern world: the leaders were paid a sum of money to salve their conscience and the trains were provided.

The evacuation of the last detachments, a squadron of the 28th Cavalry and a platoon of the Warwicks, took place quietly on April 1st. No demonstrations took place, the train with the Warwicks leaving shortly after midnight, and the cavalry filed out of the town along the road to Bajgiran early in the morning.

The attitude of the Committee remained friendly and courteous, although some members felt they had been let down and said so. Zimen alone showed signs of resentment, but at the last moment even he expressed his appreciation of what had been done for them, and intimated that he fully understood the inevitability of the British withdrawal. The Turkman leaders, who had the most to lose, remained friendly. Their relations with the British troops, especially with the Indians, had been close and harmonious, and, despite their own unreliability as soldiers and their looting propensities, they were popular with the Indian army officers, who regarded them as magnificent potential cavalry if properly trained and well led.

A considerable quantity of military stores was left at the disposal of the Committee. A strong military position, with support lines and strongpoints on the flanks protected by barbed wire, had been constructed at Annenkovo, largely under General Beatty's direction. Relations with Beatty had been good, Oraz Sirdar being disposed during the last phase to leave such matters in the hands of the British commander. The small-calibre guns on the armoured trains had been replaced by larger guns sent from Enzeli, where a quantity of artillery and ammunition had been taken from Baku at the time of the evacuation of Baku in September of the previous year. (The excuse of the Centro-Caspian government that they had insufficient war material to conduct a defence of Baku was shown to be untenable by Dunsterville's staff, who found more than fifty guns, some quite new and of Allied manufacture, and a large quantity of ammunition in various stores. Much of this was removed by Dunsterville to prevent it falling into Turkish hands.)

Oraz Sirdar and members of his staff received high decorations from the British government. The Turkman leader was to remain at his post, although superseded in the High Command by General Lazarev in April. He eventually withdrew to Persia where he lived in retirement for a year or two before his death in 1922. Several other Turkman leaders made their way to Khiva; others went to Persia or Afghanistan; a few remained until the Transcaspian force was overwhelmed by Frunze's 'Red' Army in the late summer of 1919.

The Mission, reverting to control by G.H.Q. in India, and with a reduced staff, remained in Meshed for another year. Contact was maintained with Ashkhabad until the withdrawal of the Transcaspian government to Krasnovodsk in July, but no further supplies or financial help was given. The 'Red' onslaught, executed with substantial reinforcements of 'Red' Army troops from Russia, began in May, Merv being occupied. A month later Tedzhen fell, followed by Kaakha. The Transcaspians retired to Ashkhabad, which was evacuated by the government and the army on July 15th. A new front was maintained for a time in the vicinity of Kizyl Arvat, but, with the arrival of the main body of Frunze's army in the autumn, this position was abandoned, the remnant of the Transcaspian force withdrawing to Krasnovodsk, whence the British naval detachment had already left for Enzeli. Krasnovodsk was occupied by the Bolshevik forces at the beginning of 1920, thus completing their reoccupation of the whole of Transcaspia.

21

End of a Mission

SHORTLY after the return of the Mission to Meshed the third Afghan war broke out. The assassination of the Emir Habibullah heralded the beginning of disturbances on the North-West Frontier of India and in the Punjab, where Caliphate agitation had been growing throughout 1918. Although the machinations of German and Turkish missions in Afghanistan had been unsuccessful in persuading the Emir Habibullah to throw in his lot with the Central Powers, they had succeeded in arousing the sympathies of a group of malcontents, with whom was associated the Emir's third son Amanullah. After the Emir's assassination at Jelalabad, in February 1919, Amanullah was proclaimed King and immediately declared his pan-Islamic sympathies and at the same time turned to Moscow. He addressed a letter to Lenin extolling the efforts of the Bolshevik leader in achieving freedom for the Russian people. In reply, Lenin congratulated Amanullah on having defended his people against foreign oppressors.

In May Amanullah attacked British posts on the North-West Frontier and war began. It was an unequal struggle, and within the space of eight weeks the Afghans asked for an armistice.

The early collapse of the Afghan war in August frustrated any schemes the Tashkent Soviet may have had to take advantage of the change of regime in Kabul. Suspicion on both sides prevented any agreement for mutual collaboration being reached. Some military equipment was promised by Tashkent to the Afghans but was not delivered, a circumstance which led to much mutual recrimination, which was reflected in reports which appeared in the Communist Press of Tashkent at that time, but which have since been expunged from the Soviet official record. Accusations of betrayal made by the Afghan Foreign Minister and the Afghan Consul in Tashkent hardly accorded with the fiction, since sedulously fostered, that the Afghan war was a popular revolutionary conflict, waged for 'democratic' ideals, with which the Tashkent Soviet was in sympathy. Although encouragement had been given to anti-British elements in Afghanistan, and the efforts of Indian agitators in Tashkent were supported, the Tashkent Soviet seemed hesitant in making up its mind as to which line to take. Amanullah's attack against the Anglo-Indian army on the North-West Frontier was welcomed by Moscow, but, despite the exchange of friendly correspondence between Lenin and the Afghan leader, there was no sign that the Soviet government had any illusions regarding the 'popular' and democratic nature of the new Afghan regime.

During the Afghan war the Malleson Mission in Meshed conducted 'deception' operations against both Afghan and Bolshevik, evidently with a considerable degree of success, as the uneasy relationship between Tashkent and Kabul quickly degenerated into mutual suspicion. Afghan aims in Tedzhen were made known in Tashkent, while Bolshevik repressive activity against Muslim leaders and mullas in Turkistan was brought to the attention of the population of Herat and Kandahar, already lukewarm in its attitude towards the new regime in Kabul.

After the capture of Ashkhabad by the Tashkent army considerable Bolshevik forces were concentrated in Transcaspia, and for a time it seemed likely that they might be used for an invasion of Khorosan. A revolt, led by Kurdish and local Turki-speaking elements, against the Persian central government in Tehran, spread to Khorosan and was supported and encouraged by the Soviet authorities in Transcaspia. As a result, some reinforcement of the troops at Malleson's disposal took place, mainly along the lines of communication. As the threat subsided, most of these were withdrawn to India. This small protective force, at no time exceeding some 2,000 men in all, has since been magnified in numbers and armament by Soviet historians to an army of 8,000 men, poised for a second attempt to 'invade' Turkistan and create a new colonial domain in Central Asia.[1]

Thus ended the 'Transcaspian episode'. Begun as an improvisation on characteristic British army lines, without clearly defined plan or policy, to deal with a situation as it arose, it has passed into military history as one of many such episodes, an almost forgotten campaign. The last round of the 'Great Game' had been played with the conclusion of the Anglo-Afghan war in 1919.

Yet the echoes of these events still reverberate throughout the vast region east of the Caspian, and continue to play an important part in the story of the revolutionary years as presented in Soviet accounts.

In Tashkent, Stalinabad and Alma-Ata, 'Academies of Sciences' and 'Institutes of Oriental Studies', controlled by Moscow, produce historical studies of the civil-war period which aim at perpetuating a simplified version of a very complex story—a version which ignores the realities of Turkistan Muslim nationalism—which glosses over the tragedy of Kokand, and seeks to attribute the years of revolt by the Muslim population to the machinations of British 'imperialists' and Menshevik and Socialist-Revolutionary 'traitors'. The fact that the war with the Central Powers was still in progress in 1918, and that the Turks and Germans were advancing without serious hindrance on Persia and Turkistan, is usually disregarded or minimized, as is the even more significant fact that Allied victory in the West lifted the heavy burden of the Brest-Litovsk Peace Treaty from the Soviet state, releasing its resources of men and material for the struggle against counter-revolution and national revolt.

Allied support of the 'White' reaction against the Bolshevik regime which followed the collapse of the Central Powers was brought about partly as a response to declared Bolshevik plans and agitation for world revolution, although the miscalculations and errors of the Allied representatives at Versailles played their part. Seen retrospectively, intervention and support of 'White' generals may have been a mistaken policy, but the circumstances which gave rise to intervention and support of anti-Bolshevik forces are often forgotten or ignored.

The failure of the counter-revolution was perhaps inevitable and was due to a variety of causes, among which were lack of unity among the various 'White' organizations, absence of any positive programme or appeal for popular support, and Russian suspicion of foreign intervention. There was little support at first for the Communists outside the larger cities, but Tsarism was bankrupt and the clock could not be put back. There was much popular apathy and confusion. The strong anti-Western and, in particular, anti-British sentiment of a large section of the Russian people made them suspicious and resentful of foreign interference.

The Bolsheviks alone were united and single-minded. Their original programme was simple: peace and the land to the toiler. They did not, as they have since sought to persuade themselves and the world, make the revolution. They took it over from the weak hands of the Liberals and right-wing Socialist Revolutionaries and 'Cadets', letting loose the forces of chaos and disorder. Their achievement has been the reconstruction of the state on the ruins of the old order, not on lines of Social Democracy but as a centralized autocracy on traditional Russian lines, reasserting the age-old Russian suspicion of the West, nationalism, and a new Orthodoxy, that of Marxism (in a distorted form) replacing the old Orthodoxy of Byzantium and Moscow. The traditional Tsarist instruments of control and coercion have been reimposed: the secret police, censorship, control of the printing press, the judiciary and education. While denouncing imperialism and colonialism abroad, a Soviet Russian colonial regime has been imposed by force on the 30,000,000 peoples of Central Asia and Caucasia, with sops to national sentiment in the form of encouragement of local 'culture' and the arts.

Persia, an objective of Russian expansion since the eighteenth century, is again under pressure from her northern neighbour, whose Middle Eastern policies, conducted with different slogans and greater subtlety than those of the former Imperial regime, continue to follow the traditional Russian pattern.

The Iraq revolution of 1958 has not yet run its course, the initial Communist attempt to seize control having met with a setback, which may turn out to be a case of *reculer pour mieux sauter*.

Afghanistan has become an object for Soviet economic penetration and political blandishment and a somewhat reluctant instrument for exercising pressure on a Western-oriented Pakistan.

The beginnings of this new phase in relations between East and West, particularly in the Islamic world of the Middle East and North Africa, are to be found in the convulsions and breakdown of traditional social and political forms after the First World War, set in train by the collapse of the Turkish Empire and the Caliphate and the chaotic conditions in Russian Central Asia and Caucasia which followed the seizure of power in Russia by the Bolsheviks in the grim autumn of 1917 and Russian withdrawal from the war.

After a brief and hectic period of struggle from Russian control, with the declared object of attaining national autonomy within the new

L

Russian state, the Muslim tribes of north Caucasia, the Georgians, Armenians and Azerbaijanis of Transcaucasia, and the Turko-Mongol-Persian peoples of Central Asia, were reconquered by the military forces of the Soviet inheritors of the Tsarist Russian Empire, and incorporated in the Soviet Union, nominally as self-governing republics within the Union, but in reality under the firm control of the central administration of the U.S.S.R. and the Communist party.

Central Asia has assumed a greater importance for the Soviet Union than it had been for the Tsarist Empire. For the latter it was a colony, a source of raw materials (chiefly cotton) and an area of expansion towards the natural frontier zone of the Pamirs and the Hindu Kush. For the Soviets it is a watch-tower for the East, a military base, and a show window for the peoples of the Asian and African continents, as well as an area for colonization and industrial development.[2]

Because of its political and military significance for the Middle East, and indeed for Western Asia as a whole, the region has acquired a new importance for statesmen and strategists, transcending the comparatively simple conflicts of Anglo-Russian rivalry which stemmed from British responsibility for the defence of India and from Russian expansion towards the Afghan and Persian borders and the barrier of the Pamirs. These have been replaced by the more complex problems which arise from the nationalist awakening and industrialization of Asia, and by the impact of the new Russian and Chinese imperialism that is masked under the slogans of world Communism, operating as instruments of Russian and Chinese great-power policies.

APPENDIX I

SOVIET DECLARATION OF RIGHTS TO THE PEOPLES OF RUSSIA AND MUSLIM TRIBES OF RUSSIA AND THE EAST

Pronounced at the 3rd Session of the Petrograd Soviet on November 15th, 1917

Muslims of Russia, Tartars of the Volga and the Crimea, Kirghiz, Kazakhs and Sarts of Siberia and Turkistan, Turks and Tartars of Transcaucasia, Chechens and Mountaineers of the Caucasus, and all those whose Mosques and Oratories have been destroyed, whose beliefs and customs have been trampled under foot by the Tsars and oppressors of Russia. Your beliefs and usages, your national and cultural institutions, are henceforth free and inviolate. Organize your life in complete freedom. You have the right. Know that your rights, like those of all the peoples of Russia, are under the powerful safeguard of the revolution and its organs, the Soviet of Workers, Soldiers and Peasants. Lend your support to this revolution and its government.

At a fractional Conference of the Bolshevik party held in Petrograd in April 1917 Stalin declared:

'The oppressed people comprised within Russia must be given the right to decide for themselves the question whether they want to remain within the composition of the State of Russia, or to separate and form their own independent States.'—(*Revolution and the Question of Nationalities* (Communist Academy, 1930), Vol. iii, p. 8.)

APPENDIX II

BRITISH AND INDIAN TROOPS TAKING PART IN OPERATIONS IN TRANSCASPIA, AUGUST 1918 TO APRIL 1919

1. *From August 1918 until November 1918*
   28th Indian Cavalry, two squadrons
   19th Punjabi Infantry, two companies

2. *From November 1918 until April 1919*
   28th Indian Cavalry, three squadrons
   19th Punjabi Infantry, three companies
   1/4th Hampshire Regiment, one company
   Royal Warwick Regiment, two companies
   44th Battery, Royal Field Artillery
   British and Indian details, from East Persian Cordon and
   Dunsterforce—about fifty officers and other ranks.

   Total British strength at time of evacuation: 950 officers and men.

NOTES

Chapter 1

1 See Appendix I.

2 The word *Basmachi* (robbers) was applied by the Bolsheviks in a derogatory sense to the Muslim national revolt against Russian domination and Bolshevism. There had been earlier revolts, culminating in the great rising in 1916 which had been crushed with severity by Tsarist troops. Alienation of native lands for the benefit of Russian settlers was the chief cause of anti-Russian feeling. Although suppressed by the 'Red' Army in 1924, Basmachi bands continued to operate in remote parts of Turkistan, and during the Second World War risings against Soviet authority and attacks on Russian settlers and state farms took place in Kazakhstan and Kirghizia, as well as in the Caucasus.

3 Kazemzadeh, Firuz, *The Struggle for Transcaucasia*.
Official History of the War, 1914–1918, Vol. IV, *Mesopotamia*, p. 198.

Chapter 2

1 Red Guards under Kolesov had attacked Bukhara in February 1918 but had been repulsed by the Emir's forces.

2 *Official History of the War*, Vol. IV.
Kazemzadeh, F., op. cit., p. 136.
Dunsterville, Major-General L. C., *Adventures of Dunsterforce*, Ch. XII.

3 Ullman, R. H., *Intervention and the War*, Ch. XI.

Chapter 3

1 *Official History of the War*, Vol. IV.
Kazemzadeh, F., op. cit., Ch. VIII.

2 Dunsterville, op. cit.
Kazemzadeh, op. cit., Ch. VIII.

3 Goltz, General Freiherr von der, *Zwischen Sinai und Kaukasus*.
Avalishvili, Z., *Independence of Georgia*, p. 57.

4 Avalishvili, op. cit., pp. 66–7, 115–16.

5 Kazemzadeh, op. cit., p. 135.

6 Kadischev, A. B., *Interventzia i grazhdanskaya voina v Zakavkaz'e*.

Chapter 4

1 Ullman, R. H., op. cit., Ch. XI, p. 316.

2 Ullman, R. H., op. cit., Ch. XI, p. 315.

3 *Sbornik dokumentov*, Document No. 54.
Central Asian Review, Vol. VII, No. 2 (1959), p. 117.
4 Dickson, Brigadier-General W. E., *East Persia*.
5 See Appendix I.

Chapter 5

1 Famine was largely due to the cessation of corn deliveries from European Russia. Turkistan had been forced to devote most of its irrigated area to cotton growing, and was therefore dependent on metropolitan Russia for foodstuffs.

2 Knollys, Lieutenant-Colonel A. E., *Journal of the Royal Central Asian Society*, Vol. XIII, Part 2, 1926.

Chapter 6

1 The strength of British forces engaged with the Turks in Baku was approximately 1,500. Casualties in killed and wounded were heavy.

2 Ullman, op. cit., Ch. XI, p. 320.

3 In various Soviet accounts Teague-Jones is accused of having supervised the shooting of the Commissars. He was, in fact, in Ashkhabad, several hundred miles away, and had no knowledge of Funtikov's intentions. No British officers were present at the execution of the Commissars (Kazemzadeh, op. cit., p. 145).

4 *Central Asian Review*, Vols. VI, No. 3, and VII, No. 2.

5 Kazemzadeh, op. cit., pp. 143–5.

Chapter 7

1 *Official History of the War*, Vol. IV.
2 Dickson, Brigadier-General, op. cit.

Chapter 8

1 Bailey, Lieutenant-Colonel F. M., *Mission to Tashkent*, Ch. III.

2 Most Soviet historians of the revolution in Turkistan accept the story uncritically, including Babakhodzhaev, Kuliyev and Aleskerov, but present no evidence other than press reports and hearsay.

Chapter 9

1 Aleskerov describes the battle of Dushakh as a Bolshevik victory which resulted in the withdrawal of British troops from Transcaspia (Aleskerov, *Interventzia i grazhdanskaya voina v srednei azii*, p. 109).

Chapter 10

1 Dickson, op. cit.
2 Norris, Captain D., *Caspian Naval Expedition.*
3 Kazemzadeh, op. cit., pp. 164–5.

Chapter 11

1 Ullman, op. cit., pp. 326–7.
2 Hayit, Baymirza, *Turkistan im XX Jahrhundert.*
3 *Official History of the War*, Vol. IV.

Chapter 12

1 Ullman, op. cit., p. 327.
   Ullman quotes a number of official documents and telegrams having bearing on the question of British withdrawal from Transcaspia.
2 In Soviet accounts, the issue by Malleson of promissory notes is depicted as a fraudulent scheme to extract money for the purposes of the Mission. After the withdrawal of British troops a number of forged notes appeared on the market.

Chapter 13

1 Soviet writers seem uncertain how to deal with the Tsarist period in Turkistan. At first it was treated critically as a period of Russian colonialism and exploitation. After various changes in the party line, resulting in the disappearance of exponents of earlier viewpoints, Russian occupation of Central Asia in the nineteenth century is now considered to have been in the interests of the native inhabitants. The almost continual revolts against Russian domination and Russian settlement on native lands are minimized or explained away as the work of reactionaries and fanatics.
2 Hayit, Baymirza, op. cit., Ch. II, pp. 56–60.

Chapter 14

1 Kazemzadeh, op. cit., pp. 164–6.
2 Dickson, op. cit., Ch. VI.

Chapter 15

1 Kazemzadeh, p. 165.
2 Brun, A. H., *Troublous Times.*
   Central Asian Review, Vol. IX, No. 3 (1961).

Chapter 16

1 Ullman, op. cit., Ch. XI, p. 327.

2 Knollys, op. cit.

Chapter 17

1 Kazemzadeh, op. cit., Ch. XI, pp. 253–61

2 See Appendix II.

Chapter 18

1 Hayit, op. cit., Chs. II and III.

Chapter 19

1 Ullman, op. cit., pp. 326–7.

2 Bailey, op. cit., pp. 148.

3 Hayit, op. cit., pp. 93–5.

4 Safarov, G., *Kolonialnaya Revolyutsia-opit Turkistana*, pp. 104–5.

Chapter 20

1 Frazer-Tytler, Sir W. K., *Afghanistan*.

Chapter 21

1 L. I. Miroshnikov, *Angliiskaya Ekspansia v Irane*.
  Miroshnikov, in his book published in 1961, reverts to this theme, minimizing the Turko-German threat to India and ignores the Soviet attempt to bring about a revolution in Persia. He grossly exaggerates the number of British troops in Persia between 1918 and 1920.

2 The present trend of Soviet policy in Central Asia appears to be towards unification of the nominally independent republics, with more direct and firmer control from Moscow.

BIBLIOGRAPHY

Note: Where no English version exists, a translation of the title is given in square brackets.

Aleskerov, Y., *Interventsia i grazhdanskaya voina v srednei azii* [Intervention and civil war in Central Asia], (Tashkent, 1959).

An account of British intervention in Central Asia in 1918–1919; although historically unreliable on the main issues, Aleskerov's book contains interesting material concerning the Turkistan Soviet government's relations with Bukhara and on domestic issues.

Avalishvili, Z. (Avalov), *Nezavisimost Gruzii* (Paris, 1924), English translation *Independence of Georgia* (privately published, London, 1935).

An authoritative account of the establishment of an independent regime in Georgia in 1918 and its relations with the German High Command and the Armenian and Azerbaijan nationalist governments.

Babakhodzhaev, A. K., *Proval angliiskoi aggressivnoi politiki v srednei azii, 1917–1918* [Collapse of British aggressive policy in Central Asia, 1917–1918], (Tashkent, 1935).

Although historically inaccurate, contains much interesting material relating to the Civil War period. Follows the official 'party line' of the pre-Khrushchev period.

Bailey, Lieutenant-Colonel F. M., *Mission to Tashkent* (Jonathan Cape, London, 1946).

Bennigsen, A., *La Famille musalmane en Union Sovietique* (Monde Russe et Sovietique, Paris, 1959).

Brun, A. H., *Troublous Times* (Constable, London, 1931).

Deals with the fate of the German and Austro-Hungarian prisoners of war in Russian Turkestan.

Caroe, Olaf, *Soviet Empire: The Turks of Central Asia and Stalinism* (Macmillan, London, 1953).

Central Asian Review, Vol. VIII, No. 3 (1960), and Vol. IX, No. 3 (1961), (Central Asian Research Centre, London).

Chaikin, Vadim, *K istorii rossiskoi revolyutzi* (Moscow, 1922).

An inaccurate and propagandist account of the shooting of the Twenty-Six Baku Commissars written by a member of the Socialist-Revolutionary party.

Chokaev, Mustafa, 'Turkistan in 1918', in the *Royal Central Asian Journal*, Vol. XVIII (London, 1931).

The author played an important part in the nationalist movement of the Muslim peoples of Central Asia in 1917–1918.

Churchill, W. S., *The World Crisis*, Vol. 3, Chaps. LXXXVII and CL (4 vols., Hutchinson, London, 1923–9).
In this volume of his account of the First World War, Sir Winston Churchill describes the background to the discussions in London and Paris on intervention in Russia in 1918.

Conquest, Robert, *Deportation of Soviet Nationalities* (Macmillan, London, 1960).

Dickson, Brigadier-General W. E., *East Persia* (Edward Arnold, London, 1924).

Dunsterville, Major-General L. C., *Adventures of Dunsterforce* (Edward Arnold, London, 1921).
A first-hand account of the temporary occupation of Baku by a small British force in August 1918.

Etherton, P. T., *In the Heart of Asia* (Constable, London, 1925).

Frazer-Tytler, Sir W. K., *Afghanistan* (Oxford University Press, 1950).

Goltz, General Freiherr von der, *Zwischen Sinai und Kaukasus* (Berlin, 1923).

Great Soviet Encyclopaedia (Second Edition, Moscow, 1954).
Articles on Baku, Transcaspia and the Twenty-six Commissars.

Greaves, R. L., *Persia and the Defence of India, 1884–1892* (Athlone Press, London, 1959).

Hayit, Baymirza, *Turkestan im XX Jahrhundert* (C. W. Leske Verlag, Darmstadt, 1956).
A well-documented and historically authoritative account of the rise of nationalism among the Muslim peoples of Turkistan, the attempt to set up an autonomous regime, and its suppression by the Turkistan Soviet government.

Hentig, W. von, *Ins verschlossene Land* (Berlin, 1928).

Kadishev, A. B., *Interventzia i grazhdanskaya voina v Zakavkaz'e* [Intervention and civil war in the Caucasus], (Moscow, 1960).
A reasonably objective account of military operations in Transcaucasia in 1918–1919 by an officer of the Soviet Ministry of Defence.

Kazemzadeh, Firuz, *The Struggle for Transcaucasia, 1917–1921* (G. Ronald, Oxford, 1952).
A valuable study of events in Transcaucasia during the revolutionary years, by a trained historian of Persian and Russian origin, written in a detached and objective manner; well documented.

Knollys, Lieutenent-Colonel A. E., 'Military Operations in Transcaspia', in the *Royal Central Asian Journal* (Vol. XIII, Part 2, London, 1926).

Kuliyev, K., *Borba kommunisticheskoi partii za uprochenie sovietskoi vlasti i osushchestvlenie natzional'noi politiki v srednei azii* [The struggle of the Communist Party for the consolidation of Soviet authority and the creation of a national policy in Central Asia], (Tashkent, 1956).

Lenczowski, G., *Russia and the West in Iran* (Cornell University Press, Ithaca, New York, 1949).

Malleson, Major-General Sir Wilfred, 'The British Mission in Turkistan', in the *Royal Central Asian Journal* (Vol. IX, London, 1923).

Miroshnikov, L. I., *Angliiskaya Ekspansia v Irane* [British Expansion in Persia], (Moscow, 1961).

Norris, Captain D., 'Caspian Naval Expedition', in the *Royal Central Asian Journal* (Vol. X, London, 1923).

Official History of the War, 1914–1918, Vol. IV, *Mesopotamia*, based on official documents (His Majesty's Stationery Office, London, 1924).

Park, A. G., *Bolshevism in Turkistan, 1917–1927* (Russian Institute of Columbia University, New York, 1957).

Pierce, R. A., *Russian Central Asia 1867–1917* (University of California Press, 1960).

Safarov, G., *Kolonialnaya Revolyutsia—opit Turkistana* (Moscow, 1921).

Sbornik Dokumentov: Turkistan v period inostrannoi interventsii, 1918–1919 [Collected Documents: Turkistan during the period of foreign intervention 1918–1919], (Turkistan State Publishing Office, Ashkhabad, 1957).

Shteinberg, E., *Ocherki istorii turkmenii* (Moscow, 1934).
    A frank and interesting account of Soviet colonialism and chauvinism in Central Asia by a Soviet historical writer. (Quoted by Hayit, op. cit., p. 95.)

Ullman, R. H., *Intervention and the War* (Oxford University Press, and Princeton University Press, Princeton, N.J., 1961).
    Contains hitherto unpublished material relating to British intervention in Transcaspia and the Caucasus.

White Paper, Command Paper No. 1846 (Russia No. 1) (His Majesty's Stationery Office, London, 1923).
    This White Paper contains correspondence relating to Soviet charges of British complicity in the shooting of the Twenty-six Baku Commissars in 1918.

Wilfort, F., *Turkestanisches Tagebuch* (Vienna, 1930).
    A first-hand account of experiences of an Austrian prisoner of war in Turkistan during the revolutionary years.

Zenkovsky, S. A., *Pan-Turkism and Islam in Russia* (Harvard University Press, 1960).

INDEX

Date Due